Walk like Jesus Walked

Volume 4

"You will receive Power"

A study in the Acts of the Apostles

Loren VanGalder

Spiritual Father Publications

Contents

1

The Apostles Make Four Mistakes

Acts 1:1-14

This first chapter of Acts is glorious! It's a bridge between Jesus' amazing ministry in the Gospels and the Spirit's powerful move in the early church. It's the grand finale to the most incredible life ever lived on this earth. Yes, Jesus died, but he is alive! He rose from the dead! He appeared to his disciples with unmistakable proofs that he was alive, promising something that would change their lives: The baptism in the Holy Spirit and supernatural power. Jesus completed his mission, gave the apostles the Great Commission (to make disciples of every nation), and ascended to his Father's right hand in the glory of heaven, to reign as King of the universe.

In no way do I intend to minimize those wonders, but the theme of this series is "Walk like Jesus walked." These disciples walked with Jesus for three years. You may have walked with the Lord for many years. You may have read the first books in this series and are busy making disciples in obedience to the Great Commission. Nevertheless, unfortunately, we can still make mistakes. Right in front of the risen Lord—and later, two angels— the apostles make four mistakes. Despite years of preparation

1

walking with Jesus, they betray a serious misunderstanding of his mission and the task he gave them! These first mistakes are not critical, but in the same chapter, they make their first decision as a church. Jesus is not physically with them, the angels are gone, and they still have not received the Spirit. Although there apparently were no serious consequences of it, that decision was unwise and raises doubts about whether these apostles can make it on their own. You will read about it in the next chapter.

The foundation for Acts: What Jesus did on earth

¹In my former book, Theophilus, I wrote about all that Jesus began to do and to teach ²until the day he was taken up to heaven, after giving instructions through the Holy Spirit to the apostles he had chosen. ³After his suffering, he presented himself to them and gave many convincing proofs that he was alive. He appeared to them over a period of forty days and spoke about the kingdom of God.

What Jesus began to do and teach.

The author, a doctor named Luke, is referring to his Gospel. That "former" book, like this one, was written to Theophilus. His name means "Lover of God," and he may have been a specific person, or Luke may have written for anyone who loves God.

Luke points to two things that were always part of Jesus' ministry: Words and deeds. But why does Luke say he *began* to do and teach these things? Christ indeed finished his work in this world, but he continues working today through his Body, the church. This book is a record of the apostles' words and deeds. They will do the "greater works" that Jesus said they would do (Jn. 14:12). Even though this book is titled "The Acts of the Apostles," it could be called "The *Words* and Acts of the Apostles" because they follow the Master's example—teaching and doing.

Until the day he was taken up to heaven.

The previous volume in this series talks about the importance of work. Jesus was working and serving his Father until the day he ascended to heaven.

He suffered.

Jesus did miracles and taught about the kingdom, but the primary purpose of his life was to die as a sacrifice for the forgiveness of our sins. This book will focus on what happened after his death.

He presented himself to them with many proofs that he was alive.

The proofs were convincing, leaving no doubt that he had physically risen from the dead. Compared to all he did and taught prior to this death, his ministry during these forty days was very limited: He appeared only to those who believed in him, to give them these proofs, some final instructions, and more teaching on a single theme:

Over forty days he spoke to them about the kingdom of God.

During these final days he did not cover the believer's daily life or details of how to organize the church. He spoke *only* about the kingdom, a principal topic during his three-year ministry and the subject of the second book in this series. What part does the kingdom play in your teaching and preaching?

Instructions were given to the apostles through the Holy Spirit.

Jesus said he did not say or do anything on his own initiative. Even these instructions were given through the Holy Spirit, the same Spirit who would soon baptize the apostles, who powerfully manifests himself in this book, and inspires us today to speak about and do the work of the kingdom. Luke makes it clear that Jesus chose the apostles.

The apostles continue what Jesus began to do and teach.

That is the theme of Acts. Jesus only laid the foundation. He is the chief cornerstone. Now it is up to the apostles to establish the church, doing Jesus' works and teaching his word.

The final instruction: Wait

The NIV places this command in the context of a meal, although that detail is not clear in the Greek. What is certain is that meals and the time shared around the table were important to Jesus. In Galilee, he prepared breakfast on the beach for them (Jn. 21). Although we cannot be sure they were eating, they were definitely together.

⁴ On one occasion, while he was eating with them, he gave them this command: "Do not leave Jerusalem, but wait for the gift my Father promised, which you have heard me speak about. ⁵ For John baptized with water, but in a few days you will be baptized with the Holy Spirit."

It would be disastrous for them to leave the fellowship and relative security of Jerusalem without the baptism of the Holy Spirit. You might wonder:

- Shouldn't three years of discipleship with God's Son be enough?
- Aren't three years in a Bible institute enough?
- He had breathed on them and said, *"Receive the Holy Spirit"* (Jn. 20:22). What more did they need?

They need what the Father promised

This baptism is not optional or only for some super-spiritual believers. We do not have to beg the Father for it. It is a promise.

What we have to do is wait. God promises us many things, but we do not get everything at once; we have to wait for many of them. In this case, it would not be a long wait; it would be within a few days.

Jesus compares this filling with John's baptism, a baptism of repentance—distinct from the believers' baptism in water, which Jesus commanded in the Great Commission. This baptism is not in water, but in the Holy Spirit—it is an immersion, a filling, of the Spirit.

Are you baptized in the Holy Spirit? If you are, you will give a confident and joyful "yes!" Too often, I hear these responses:

- "Sure…I think so."
- "Somebody told me every believer is filled with the Spirit."
- "I don't go to a Pentecostal church."
- "I was baptized in water, and they said the Spirit would come on me at the same time."
- "Of course. I go to a Pentecostal church." However, I know many—perhaps the majority—in Pentecostal or charismatic churches who have not been baptized in the Holy Spirit.

The excuses really are not important. I am not concerned with what you call it. It is not the purpose of this book to promote a particular doctrine about how to receive the Holy Spirit. What we can say and believe is clearly presented in the Book of Acts: The power and presence of the Spirit in your life is essential. Some call this book "The Acts of the Holy Spirit," because it is the Spirit who did the work in the early church. This is the Father's promise to you. God wants to baptize you in his Spirit.

⁶ Then they gathered around him and asked him, "Lord, are you at this time going to restore the kingdom to Israel?"

⁷ He said to them: "It is not for you to know the times or dates the Father has set by his own authority.

After all he had taught them about the kingdom of heaven, Jesus could feel very discouraged to realize they had missed the message. They were still thinking in this world. They totally overlooked God's glorious promise, just as many Christians today miss the blessing of the Spirit because they are so focused on prosperity and worldly blessings. While Jesus spoke to them about the kingdom, they were thinking about the past, when Israel was a mighty nation, and about independence from Rome. Yes, their response could be discouraging, but Jesus knew a secret: soon the Spirit would come and reveal many truths about the kingdom to them. Meanwhile, Jesus was left to correct their mistakes.

Three mistakes

1. They asked if Jesus was going to *"restore"* the kingdom. They were thinking about a physical kingdom, but God's kingdom is spiritual! It is not of this world! His kingdom will be fully established when Christ returns. Through the centuries, many have attempted to establish a physical kingdom on this earth, and they have always been disappointed. It cannot work. There is a strong tendency in today's church to embrace this same error.

2. They were thinking about a specific nation or group of people who would reign. Jesus responds that the kingdom includes the despised Samaritans and people from every nation and race. The perversion of what Christ intends for his kingdom has given rise to the

tragedy of all kinds of racism, prejudice, and abuse, even in the church.

3. They want the kingdom now, "*at this time.*" While it is true that we can experience many of its benefits now, the kingdom will gradually grow until Christ comes to establish it physically. Much patience and faith are required to hold onto that vision of the kingdom and persevere amid the world's opposition. There are many books, YouTube videos, and Internet pages devoted to discussing the antichrist, the great tribulation, and when Christ will return. People always try to set dates, but it is not for us to know those details. I have heard people say: "Jesus spoke about not knowing the day or the hour, but we can know the month or the year." They are missing Jesus' clear message. We do need to observe what is going on in the world and respond with wisdom, but most of these things must be left in God's hands. There are more pressing things for us.

What is most important: Receive power and be witnesses

⁸ But you will receive power when the Holy Spirit comes on you; and you will be my witnesses in Jerusalem, and in all Judea and Samaria, and to the ends of the earth."

This is what we should be about: being Christ's witnesses, or, in other words, obeying the Great Commission. We cannot do that without the Spirit's power. Do you have that power? If you are baptized in the Spirit and have his power, you will witness about Jesus. He will give you many opportunities. It will be natural—not something scary or left to "evangelists." The Spirit will send us to the ends of the earth. If you feel like you do not have that power and rarely witness about Jesus, examine yourself to see if you are baptized in the Spirit.

The ascension

⁹ After he said this, he was taken up before their very eyes, and a cloud hid him from their sight.

¹⁰ They were looking intently up into the sky as he was going, when suddenly two men dressed in white stood beside them. ¹¹ "Men of Galilee," they said, "why do you stand here looking into the sky? This same Jesus, who has been taken from you into heaven, will come back in the same way you have seen him go into heaven."

They are in shock. They were not expecting this. Those were his last words to them. Jesus ascended to his Father and, at this moment, is reigning in heaven at his right hand. When it says he will come back "*in the same way,*" it does not mean he will come to the Mount of Olives or will only come to a group of eleven apostles. In the same way he went up, he will come in a cloud, but every eye will see him (Rev. 1:7).

Do you have that hope of Christ's return? It is beautiful, yet we do not focus on that, but on the task Jesus left us to complete.

Fourth error

The disciples were left open-mouthed, staring at the sky, and the angels were incredulous. Hadn't they heard what Jesus said? Some Christians are gazing at the sky. They want nothing to do with this world, but the world needs Jesus, and in this book we will see the power we have been given to transform it.

The apostles risked two extremes: being overly focused on this world (restoring a political kingdom to Israel), and being too focused on heaven (staring at the sky instead of doing God's work). There is a healthy balance, knowing that we are citizens of heaven with the hope of eternal life, but taking advantage of every opportunity to preach and establish God's kingdom in this world.

Back to Jerusalem

¹² Then the apostles returned to Jerusalem from the hill called the Mount of Olives, a Sabbath day's walk from the city. ¹³ When they arrived, they went upstairs to the room where they were staying. Those present were Peter, John, James and Andrew; Philip and Thomas, Bartholomew and Matthew; James son of Alphaeus and Simon the Zealot, and Judas son of James.

A Sabbath day's walk was about a kilometer, less than a mile. Can you imagine what they were feeling on their way back to Jerusalem? This time they were not hopeless, but were marveling at what they had seen. They shared the experience with the women, Jesus' family, and the other disciples, about 120 in all. They alternated between time in the Upper Room and the temple: *And they stayed continually at the temple, praising God* (Lk. 24:53).

¹⁴ They all joined together constantly in prayer, along with the women and Mary the mother of Jesus, and with his brothers.

Jesus' brothers, who previously mocked him, now believe. They all obey Jesus and wait, together, in the same spirit, and devoted to prayer. It is good advice for a church today that wants to receive the power and baptism of the Holy Spirit. They obey that part, but then they add something Jesus never mentioned. We often do it: Add things to the ministry or requirements that Jesus never intended. In the next chapter, we will see the disciples' fifth mistake.

2

An Error Committed While Acting in the Flesh

Acts 1:15–26

Many look at the Bible through lenses—lenses formed by what they have heard from a priest, pastor, or YouTube. Lenses shaped by the books they have read. Now we want to remove those lenses and let the Holy Spirit speak to us. When we open the Bible, we want to read the word itself. There are study Bibles written by famous pastors. The danger is reading their notes and not letting the Spirit speak to you. Their comments are not inspired scripture. After reading, praying, and reflecting, we can read various translations to better discern the meaning of the passage. It is always good to have a notebook to record your observations or questions. Then we can read various commentaries, from various perspectives, not just the ones that you agree with. Guided by the Spirit, we make our interpretation and always make a personal application. Studying the Bible is never just an intellectual exercise; we want to let the Word shape us and transform our lives.

The case here is not closed. The best scholars disagree. Some believe Peter did the right thing. Others believe he did not, and I am with them. I am not dogmatic about it; I could be mistaken. Let's study the passage, then I will share my conclusions, and you can make your own. Whatever you think, keep reading; this is not something of critical importance.

15 In those days Peter stood up among the believers (a group numbering about a hundred and twenty).

This is Peter's first recorded discourse. It is not surprising that he would take the initiative. It could be that he was tired of praying and waiting. Remember, it was Peter in John 21 who wanted to go back to fishing because Jesus had not shown up. It is hard to wait. We want to do something. The danger is doing something that is not God's will (as in the famous passage in Matthew 7:21–23).

16 He said, "Brothers and sisters, the Scripture had to be fulfilled in which the Holy Spirit spoke long ago through David concerning Judas, who served as guide for those who arrested Jesus. 17 He was one of our number and shared in our ministry."

Peter starts right, citing the Bible. Judas' betrayal and suicide must have been traumatic for the disciples. He was one of them. They had spent three years in close fellowship. They took part in the same ministry: preaching, healing, and casting out demons. Surely there was a mix of anger, sadness, and confusion about what he did. Peter may have been reflecting on that as he prayed, and this Scripture came to mind. We do not always have to share everything the Lord reveals to us, but, being Peter, he does.

Luke adds an explanation of Judas' death:

18 (With the payment he received for his wickedness, Judas bought a field; there he fell headlong, his body burst open and all his intestines spilled out. ¹⁹*Everyone in Jerusalem heard about this, so they called that field in their language Akeldama, that is, Field of Blood.)*

It could appear to contradict Matthew 27:5: *So Judas threw the money into the temple and left. Then he went away and hanged himself.* However, it may be that when he hanged himself (or shortly thereafter), his body fell and burst open. By any measure, it was an ugly death, but the wages of sin is always death, and Judas is a good example of the consequences of denying or betraying Jesus, or being blinded by riches.

²⁰ *"For," said Peter, "it is written in the Book of Psalms:*

> *"'May his place be deserted;*
> *let there be no one to dwell in it,'*

Peter cites Psalm 69, verse 25, which speaks of God's enemies and curses them, asking God to punish them. Various gospel references apply this Psalm to Christ, including one by Jesus himself (Jn. 15:25).

> *and, "'May another take his place of leadership.'*

This is verse 8 of Psalm 109, also written by David, and is another plea for God to judge his enemies. As with various Old Testament texts cited in the New Testament, they seem out of context and do not really apply to Judas. Today, it is still common to cite verses supporting what a person believes or wants to do, disregarding the context and sound interpretation.

²¹ *Therefore it is necessary to choose one of the men who have been with us the whole time the Lord Jesus was living among us,* ²² *beginning from John's baptism to the time when Jesus was taken up from us. For one of these must become a witness with us of his resurrection."*

Peter concludes by proposing a response to Judas' death: Choose a new apostle. He gives three very clear qualifications:

1. He must be a witness of the resurrection.
2. He must have accompanied them the entire time Jesus was with them.
3. That time frame is from Jesus' baptism by John until his recent ascension.

Not many people would fulfill all those requirements; possibly one of the Seventy that Jesus also sent out. They appear nowhere else as qualifications for an apostle, and they were partially responsible for Paul's continual struggle to defend his apostleship—he met none of these requirements. Jesus never mentioned them as qualifications of an apostle.

23 So they nominated two men: Joseph called Barsabbas (also known as Justus) and Matthias. 24 Then they prayed, "Lord, you know everyone's heart. Show us which of these two you have chosen 25 to take over this apostolic ministry, which Judas left to go where he belongs." 26 Then they cast lots, and the lot fell to Matthias; so he was added to the eleven apostles.

Just as with Peter's persuasive influence in John 21 when they went fishing, there is no argument from the others. We do not know how many met the qualifications, but they propose two. After choosing them, they pray and present the two options to Jesus in prayer. Then they cast lots to determine God's will.

So why do I think they acted in the flesh?
1. Jesus never said anything about choosing another apostle. It was Jesus who designated the original Twelve, and it is his Spirit who calls, confirms, and sends apostles in the church. Acts 1:2 emphasizes that it was Jesus who chose the apostles. If he wanted someone to take Judas'

place, surely he would have chosen him during the forty days following his resurrection.

2. They did pray, but they had already chosen the two candidates. They prayed *after* deciding to name another apostle. We see it all the time: we make a decision and pray that God would bless it. Or we offer God some options, instead of entrusting the entire situation to him. For something this important, it should have been very clear that God wanted it.

3. Casting lots was common in the Old Testament, but only during the first years of Israel's history was it presented in a positive light (Lev. 16:8, Num. 26:55, and Josh. 7:14 and 18:6). None of those examples involved something of great spiritual importance. The later examples were by ungodly men: King Saul in 1 Samuel 14:42, the sailors in Jonah 1:7, Haman in Esther, and the soldiers at Jesus' crucifixion. It was never used during Jesus' ministry or after Pentecost. The model is to pray together, wait for a word from God, and then reach a unanimous decision.

4. Peter supported his plan with Scriptures taken totally out of context, and they contradict each other! One says that *nobody* would take his place, the second says that *another* would fill his place. Which is it?

5. We never hear anything more about Matthias. There are indeed others of the Twelve who do not appear in Acts, but, oddly, he is never mentioned, not even in first-century apocryphal books.

6. When James died several years later, nothing was done to name another apostle to take his place.

7. Many believe that Paul was God's choice. The fruits of that choice confirm it. Peter and the others did not want to wait for God's time.

God did not rebuke them; he seemed to ignore what they did, knowing that the Holy Spirit would soon baptize and transform them. However, several things can happen when we act in the flesh:

1. We may hurt the person chosen, in this case, Matthias. We give him false hope and a calling that is not of God.
2. We offer a poor example to young believers.
3. We may cause conflicts, such as between Paul and the other apostles.

What do you think? Was it a mistake? I may be wrong, but I believe their experience offers several things worthy of our reflection as we lead Jesus' church. It reminds me of God's complaint against Israel in Hosea 8:4: *They set up kings without my consent; they choose princes without my approval.* I do not want to fall into Israel's error, or do something in the flesh as important as choosing an apostle.

What applications can we make from this passage?

- If you are a pastor or leader, you have a great responsibility to guide your people well. Wait on the Lord for his will. Be very careful not to use questionable things, such as casting lots, to discern God's will. And have the humility to confess mistakes and receive correction from the Lord or others.
- If you are a follower and see something that seems wrong, feel free to question the pastor or leader. They are not infallible. With humility, you can question a decision that seems to go against the word of God.
- Learn how to interpret the Word of God correctly.

3

Supernatural Power

Acts 2

The goal of these four books has been to walk like Jesus walked. The apostles were not off to an encouraging start; we have already seen four mistakes they made on the day of Jesus' ascension, and one shortly thereafter. Are these really world-changers? Well, they were missing the most important ingredient in a Christ-like life: The Holy Spirit. I want to make a very simple, but radical, proposal: Why not follow the example of the early church? It is the premise of this final volume of the series: You can do what these first believers did. Of course, God was establishing the church in those days, but if he did it 2000 years ago, why can't he do it today? Isn't it needed even more? I think so.

In Acts 2, we find three things that will completely transform your life and your church. The word that summarizes this chapter is "supernatural;" it is God's sovereign work. Do you want a supernatural life? Do you believe that God can supernaturally move in your life, and wants to? Get ready for something powerful.

First step: Everyone filled with the Spirit
¹When the day of Pentecost came, they were all together in one place.

17

The disciples obeyed Jesus' command to wait for the power of the Spirit. God works when we are together, united, and committed to obeying him. The brother who did not feel like going to the Upper Room that morning did not receive the Holy Spirit.

2 Suddenly a sound like the blowing of a violent wind came from heaven and filled the whole house where they were sitting. 3 They saw what seemed to be tongues of fire that separated and came to rest on each of them. 4 All of them were filled with the Holy Spirit and began to speak in other tongues as the Spirit enabled them.

This was 100% God's sovereign move. True, they had their part in it: They were together, they were expectant, and they were in prayer. However, they did nothing to facilitate the tongues, and there was no special music or apostle who prayed for them.

The multitude who were not genuinely committed to Christ was already gone; the 120 who were left were true believers. When God moves in this way, it is for the whole church:

- The wind filled the *whole* house
- The tongues of fire rested on *each* of them.
- *All* were filled with the Spirit.
- *All* of them spoke in other tongues.

God was totally in control. Coming from heaven as tongues of fire, the Spirit took hold of them and enabled them to speak.

Tongues

A thorough study of tongues would be beneficial, but not for this book. This gift has been very controversial. Many who want to speak in tongues do not. Some say it is the essential sign of the baptism in the Spirit, based in part on these verses, but the Bible never says that it is the only sign. In 1 Corinthians, Paul says that he speaks in tongues more than any of them (14:18), and wishes they all spoke in tongues (14:5), but worship services in Corinth were chaotic, with everyone speaking in tongues at once. They had turned a gift meant to facilitate communication with God into a source of pride. Paul calls them angelic languages; we should pray in English (with the mind), but also with the Spirit, in tongues (1 Cor. 14:14–15). It is a prayer language; when I do not know how to pray, the Spirit prays for me.

I have witnessed considerable manipulation to help people speak in tongues, like rapidly repeating "hallelujah." Sometimes, if a person supposedly speaks in tongues once, they say: "Praise God, he received the baptism"—but they may never speak in tongues again! It is common to initially question whether it is of God or not. Like any language, we have to practice and develop this angelic tongue.

The baptism in the Spirit
What is really important here is not the tongues, but the baptism in the Holy Spirit. What can we say about this baptism?

- It is biblical. Jesus and the Father both promised it. Christ said he would not leave us as orphans, but would come to us (Jn. 14:18).
- It can be a sovereign outpouring, but often we have to ask for it: "*If you then, though you are evil, know how to give good gifts to your children, how much more will your Father in heaven give the Holy Spirit to those who ask him!*" (Lk. 11:13) God wants to give you his Spirit. Ask him!
- This baptism is essential to experience the life of the early church.

- It is often a powerful experience, in which you lose control of your tongue and begin to praise God in another language.

I received the baptism alone. I was reading a book called <u>Power in Praise</u>, and started to praise God in English. Suddenly I was praising in another tongue and felt waves of God's love and presence washing over me. My life was changed:

- I couldn't spend enough time in prayer and worship.
- The Bible came alive like never before.
- God gave me many opportunities to witness about my faith.
- There was new power to resist sin and temptation.

Have you experienced Pentecost like these believers?

⁵ Now there were staying in Jerusalem God-fearing Jews from every nation under heaven. ⁶ When they heard this sound, a crowd came together in bewilderment, because each one heard their own language being spoken. ⁷ Utterly amazed, they asked: "Aren't all these who are speaking Galileans? ⁸ Then how is it that each of us hears them in our native language? ⁹ Parthians, Medes and Elamites; residents of Mesopotamia, Judea and Cappadocia, Pontus and Asia, ¹⁰ Phrygia and Pamphylia, Egypt and the parts of Libya near Cyrene; visitors from Rome ¹¹ (both Jews and converts to Judaism); Cretans and Arabs—we hear them declaring the wonders of God in our own tongues!"

Known languages?

God poured out his Spirit at a perfect time: People from around the world were in Jerusalem for the feast of Pentecost (the Feast of Weeks). The commotion in that Upper Room was heard all over the city. They did not have to announce a church service, pay for publicity, or beg people to come.

I believe there were two miracles that day: in the believers' tongues, and in the ears of the crowd. Many have said that the disciples were speaking known languages, from all the countries mentioned, but three times it says, *"we hear them speak."* That is why they were bewildered and amazed! Do a simple experiment: Take 120 people, speaking loud enough to attract a crowd. Fifteen distinct groups are mentioned here; if 120 people are speaking 15 languages at the same time, nothing could be understood. God did a miracle of translation for each person!

¹² Amazed and perplexed, they asked one another, "What does this mean?" ¹³ Some, however, made fun of them and said, "They have had too much wine."

The world will be amazed and perplexed when it sees a truly Spirit-filled church. We are so joyful and under the Spirit's influence that we appear drunk!

The first step to the supernatural life Christ wants for you is to wait for, seek, and receive the baptism of the Holy Spirit.

Second step: Preach the Gospel
Somebody has to tell people what is going on. God sovereignly baptized the believers. Nobody laid hands on them, preached to them, or prayed for them. God could give the message of salvation to someone in a vision or a dream, or through an angel, but he almost always uses us. God calls us to evangelize. What a sin to say nothing to all the people gathered there!

¹⁴ Then Peter stood up with the Eleven, raised his voice and addressed the crowd: "Fellow Jews and all of you who live in Jerusalem, let me explain this to you; listen carefully to what I say.

This is the same Peter who, some fifty-three days earlier, had denied knowing Jesus out of fear of the Jews. Only two weeks before, he was ready to give up and go back to fishing. But now he is filled with the Spirit and boldness, and preaches with anointing.

Joel's prophecy fulfilled

15 These people are not drunk, as you suppose. It's only nine in the morning! 16 No, this is what was spoken by the prophet Joel:

17 "'In the last days, God says,
I will pour out my Spirit on all people.
Your sons and daughters will prophesy,
your young men will see visions,
your old men will dream dreams.
18 Even on my servants, both men and women,
I will pour out my Spirit in those days,
and they will prophesy.
19 I will show wonders in the heavens above
and signs on the earth below,
blood and fire and billows of smoke.
20 The sun will be turned to darkness
and the moon to blood
before the coming of the great and glorious day of the Lord.
21 And everyone who calls
on the name of the Lord will be saved.'

Peter preached God's Word. Our preaching must be from the Bible. Peter cites Joel's prophecy, which still applies to us:

- It is something new and different for these last days: God will pour out his Spirit on all flesh. In the Old Testament, only a few kings and prophets received the Spirit; now it is for every believer.
- Prophecy, visions, and dreams should be part of our experience. God wants to reveal himself and communicate with us.

22 *"Fellow Israelites, listen to this: Jesus of Nazareth was a man accredited by God to you by miracles, wonders and signs, which God did among you through him, as you yourselves know.* 23 *This man was handed over to you by God's deliberate plan and foreknowledge; and you, with the help of wicked men, put him to death by nailing him to the cross.* 24 *But God raised him from the dead, freeing him from the agony of death, because it was impossible for death to keep its hold on him.*

David prophesies the Messiah

Once again, he turns to the Scriptures, citing a Psalm written by the beloved King David:

25 *David said about him:*

> *"'I saw the Lord always before me.*
> *Because he is at my right hand,*
> *I will not be shaken.*
> 26 *Therefore my heart is glad and my tongue rejoices;*
> *my body also will rest in hope,*
> 27 *because you will not abandon me to the realm of the dead,*
> *you will not let your holy one see decay.*
> 28 *You have made known to me the paths of life;*
> *you will fill me with joy in your presence.'*

29 *"Fellow Israelites, I can tell you confidently that the patriarch David died and was buried, and his tomb is here to this day.* 30 *But he was a prophet and knew that God had promised him on oath that he would place one of his descendants on his throne.* 31 *Seeing what was to come, he spoke of the resurrection of the Messiah, that he was not abandoned to the realm of the dead, nor did his body see decay.* 32 *God has raised this Jesus to life, and we are all witnesses of it.* 33 *Exalted to the right hand of God, he has received from the Father the promised Holy*

Spirit and has poured out what you now see and hear. ³⁴ For David did not ascend to heaven, and yet he said,

> *"'The Lord said to my Lord:*
> *"Sit at my right hand*
> *³⁵ until I make your enemies*
> *a footstool for your feet."'*

³⁶ "Therefore let all Israel be assured of this: God has made this Jesus, whom you crucified, both Lord and Messiah."

What do we observe about his preaching?

1. It was very simple; today, we want complex and impressive preaching.
2. The focus was Jesus; he exalts Christ. Peter did not talk about his experience with Christ or how he walked on the water. Today, it is common for a preacher to draw attention to himself and entertain the people. I often have to ask myself: Where is Christ in this message?
3. He preached the Bible and explained what the Bible says; today, I often hear one or two verses read and then the Bible barely mentioned.
4. It was a short sermon; today's sermons can be painfully long.
5. He was obviously not trying to please the people; he was unafraid to put the guilt for Jesus' death on the Jews. Many preachers today are afraid to talk about topics such as sin, repentance, and holiness.

Great evangelists do not bring new revelation, but speak with the Spirit's anointing and let the Spirit do the work. Peter did not have to plead with them; the Spirit was moving in their hearts:

³⁷ When the people heard this, they were cut to the heart and said to Peter and the other apostles, "Brothers, what shall we do?"

38 Peter replied, "Repent and be baptized, every one of you, in the name of Jesus Christ for the forgiveness of your sins. And you will receive the gift of the Holy Spirit. 39 The promise is for you and your children and for all who are far off—for all whom the Lord our God will call." 40 With many other words he warned them; and he pleaded with them, "Save yourselves from this corrupt generation."

How to respond to the message

What should we tell someone who wants to accept Christ and be saved? What do they have to do?

- Repent
- Be baptized and receive forgiveness for their sins
- Expect that they will receive the gift of the Holy Spirit

Peter does not talk about prosperity, blessings, and how God is going to resolve all their problems, but rather about repentance, baptism in water, and the filling of the Holy Spirit.

41 Those who accepted his message were baptized, and about three thousand were added to their number that day.

God knew that the apostles were prepared for the church to grow and would be able to care for all these new converts. In just one day, the church grew from 120 to over 3000. Is that possible today? Why not? When the Spirit has complete freedom, we should see many conversions. I am not talking about taking people from other churches; God is going to *add* new believers. It is a huge responsibility to care for all of them, and that is the third part. We do not want to waste the harvest. We want disciples, not decisions. Jesus commanded us to make disciples.

Third step: Supernatural fellowship

42 They devoted themselves to the apostles' teaching and to fellowship, to the breaking of bread and to prayer.

Here are four essential characteristics of a Spirit-filled church:

- A foundation in sound biblical doctrine. They teach, preach, and study the Bible.
- Enjoying rich fellowship with each other.
- Sharing the Lord's Supper to remind themselves that Jesus is the center of the church. It may include sharing a meal together.
- Praying together.

43 Everyone was filled with awe at the many wonders and signs performed by the apostles.

The nature of the church is supernatural: Signs, wonders, deliverance, and healing should be a regular part of our experience. When God starts to deliver addicts and the demon oppressed, when he heals well-known people in the community, the news will spread rapidly. And when God moves that way, people will be in awe (or, as in the Greek, filled with fear). They know God is real and respect those who serve him.

44 All the believers were together and had everything in common. 45 They sold property and possessions to give to anyone who had need.

This is radical fellowship. When people are ready to give up their money and material goods, you know something profound is going on. There was equality among the believers. The wealthy sold their possessions and gave to the needy, inside and outside the church. No one was in need. Those material things just were not that important; Christ was their whole life! This is truly radical, and something rarely seen today.

When the Spirit fills us, we want to be with other Christians. Not just on Sunday and midweek; they were together all week:

[46] *Every day they continued to meet together in the temple courts. They broke bread in their homes and ate together with glad and sincere hearts,* [47] *praising God and enjoying the favor of all the people. And the Lord added to their number daily those who were being saved.*

What else characterizes a living, healthy, Spirit-filled church?

- They met together every day. When I ministered on university campuses and in prisons, I saw the vast difference that daily meetings make in a church. A couple of hours on Sunday simply is not enough to maintain the Christian life.
- They were *"in one accord"* (ASV). Far more than just being together, they were united in spirit. There was no arguing or fighting. They experienced the unity that comes from sharing the same Spirit. That is something we cannot make happen by our efforts.
- They shared meals in each other's homes.
- Glad and sincere hearts characterized them.
- They praised God.
- They enjoyed the favor of all the people, inside and outside the church. They were known for their honesty, sincerity, and generosity.
- People were naturally attracted to them. They wanted the same thing! It's powerful! Every day, the Lord added more people to the church.

Aren't those the very things we long for in a church?

Don't go back to the law!

Be careful! We cannot program this. We do not organize home meetings and pressure people to attend. We do not fill the schedule with daily worship services. We do not push people to sell their homes or give more. That is the law. That is the Old Testament. If we fall back into the law, we will quench the Spirit and destroy what Christ wants to do in the church. When we are filled with the Spirit, these things will happen naturally. We want to pray with our brothers and sisters, and look forward to more time with them. God brings us people to share the Gospel with. Everything flows from the Spirit.

Does this chapter remind you of your experience in church? Or perhaps bring back memories of what you experienced years ago? If it doesn't, could that explain why you find church boring and wonder at times if God is real? Could Acts provide you and your church with a model to follow?

4

"What I have, I give you."

Acts 3

Wow. What a start. Overnight, the church exploded to include thousands of believers full of the Holy Spirit – and it kept growing! Joy, love, and power were overflowing. Everybody loved them. What could possibly stop this revival? What should the apostles do next? How can they keep it going? They did not sit down and plan special programs. They just stayed faithful and walked like Jesus walked, doing what their Master did. Jesus never commanded us to build cathedrals or start programs; he commanded us to make disciples, heal the sick, deliver the demonized, preach the Gospel, and love others.

The disciples had learned that when we follow Jesus, he prepares the way. That is good advice for you when you are not sure what to do: Stay in church, in fellowship with other believers, and in prayer. It is an exciting life, full of surprises.

Routines
¹Now Peter and John went up together to the temple at the hour of prayer, the ninth hour (three in the afternoon). (NKJV)

Together. There it is again. At Pentecost, the believers were *together.* Now Peter and John went up to the temple *together.* God wants to deliver us from our loneliness, to walk together with other brothers and sisters. God created us for genuine friendship and fellowship; to have someone who will walk with you, not just physically, but united in heart and soul.

Every day they went up to the temple at 3 PM to pray together. It was their routine. Yes, church can become a routine, but there are good routines. For many years, the foundation of my spiritual life has been the time I spend alone with the Lord every morning. I am glad I was encouraged as a new believer to develop that routine. At first, I thought that if I missed that quiet time, the day was ruined, but God understands and is merciful. I do not do it legalistically. I do it every morning because I long for that fellowship with my Lord and Savior. I go to church because I am part of that body, and I want to worship God with them, hear the Word, and spend time with my brothers and sisters. It does not depend on my feelings, the weather, or who else goes to church. There will be times when we are sick or something unusual happens, and we cannot make it to church, but church and quiet time are routines I always want to keep. That is the way it was for Peter and John—3 PM was an hour set apart for communion with God and others in the temple.

² Now a man who was lame from birth was being carried to the temple gate called Beautiful, where he was put every day to beg from those going into the temple courts.

It was called the "Beautiful Gate," but it was not beautiful for that man. There are people in church who are going through rough times; it is hard to keep smiling and saying "Praise God" in the face of sickness, depression, or family problems. I live in a beautiful country that has been called one of the happiest countries in the world. The atmosphere is great, but that can make the depressed person feel even worse. The Beautiful Gate was a daily reminder to this man that he was not beautiful. In fact, he could not even go into the temple because of his disability; the Jews felt it was the result of his or his parents' sin, or some curse.

Thank God, nobody has to stay out of the church today. I have been in churches that are clearly for the "beautiful people." Their building has beautiful doors and comfortable seats (cushioned, of course). It is not sinful to have a beautiful building, but the church is for everyone—I have seen posted on some churches: "Sinners welcome here." Do people who are disabled, poor, or looked down on feel welcome in your church?

Somebody brought this man and left him at the temple gate every day, which means that Peter and John must have passed him many times. Even Jesus must have seen him there, but for some reason, God's time for him had not come yet. You may feel like that man. You go to church hoping to receive something. The worship leader is praising God and talks about Jesus' presence. Others get their miracles, but it seems like your turn never comes. Keep going to church. Jesus is your best hope.

Thank God for people who bring someone like this man to church, whether physically, in prayer, or through emotional support. Often it is a spouse or a parent. Was there someone who brought you to church? Thank God for that person! What is bad is to be disabled and have no one to take care of you. The good news is that Jesus knows you and loves you. If you have experienced the Lord's touch, you can be his instrument to bring someone to church, or even better, be a Peter or John for them.

This man had a routine, but it was not a good routine. He had to beg to survive. It was the only life he knew. We can mean well, but in our ignorance, we may keep someone in an unhealthy routine, like this man's friends did. It is better to teach a man how to fish than to give him a fish. You may be able to help someone recognize and break a routine that is not helping him, and bring him to Jesus. The Lord wants much more for this man than to be begging every day.

Thank God for this man's perseverance; Jesus taught about its importance in prayer. I am sure there were days when he wanted to die or even take his own life, but every day he went to the temple. Every day we need to come into the Holy Place, in God's presence, and ask for his help in our needs.

Look intently
³ When he saw Peter and John about to enter, he asked them for money.

As usual, Peter and John were probably anxious to get to the prayer on time and were not thinking about this man. We can be so used to seeing someone in our neighborhood or on the street that they almost become invisible, and we do not see their need. Peter and John were going to enter the temple without giving the man anything.

⁴ Peter and John looked at him intently, and Peter said, "Look at us!" (NLT)

Just like we often do not see the needy person, many times they do not see us. When he asked them for money, the Spirit touched something in Peter. While they looked at him intently, I believe God spoke to them that he wanted to heal him, and gave them the faith to command a healing. We do not always walk down the street commanding a healing for every sick person, just like we do not do that in a hospital, but when God speaks to us about something he wants to do, we must obey him.

Look at the people you meet during the day. Now, more than ever, many have their eyes glued to their phones. It is almost rare to make eye contact and have that connection. It costs nothing to look someone in the eyes, smile, and say "Good morning" or "God bless you." It is even more important to greet our Christian brothers and sisters. Too often, two people from the same church pass each other on the street and say nothing.

Look at them intently. Fix your eyes on them. Be sensitive to the Spirit and what he may reveal to you about them. It is not uncommon to receive a word of knowledge at that moment.

⁵ So the man gave them his attention, expecting to get something from them.

He reminds me of my dog: If he thinks he is going to get something, he becomes very attentive. The lame man had low expectations; he was only asking for a few coins to get through another day. Everybody wants to get something. We can offer them something to get their attention; as believers in Jesus Christ, it is more blessed to give than to receive. Many people leave a church because "I'm not receiving anything there." Of course, it is important to receive support and spiritual nourishment, but sometimes we have to think: "What can I give?"

What I have I give you

⁶ Then Peter said, "Silver and gold I do not have, but what I do have I give you: In the name of Jesus Christ of Nazareth, rise up and walk." (NKJV)

The man did not ask for healing. There was no evidence of faith. Peter did not say: "Can I pray for you? Maybe God will heal you." No, with his faith, he commanded him to rise up and walk. It was just as if Christ himself were there. There is power in Jesus' name to heal. Do you have the faith to command a lame man to get up and walk? Do you have the ears to hear the Spirit say: "I want to heal that man"?

Curiously, Peter and John had no money. Of course, it is common to lie to a beggar and say we do not have money when we do, but I do not think Peter was lying. He was the lead apostle, but they were poor, despite the previous chapter saying people sold their homes to give the money to the poor. Jesus never asked anyone for money, and never gave money to anyone. He was not comfortable handling money. The disciples had money; their treasurer was the infamous Judas Iscariot, who stole money and betrayed Jesus for thirty pieces of silver.

It does not matter if you do not have money. You have something much more important, which costs nothing. Lack of silver or gold should never keep you from ministering in Jesus' name. Are you willing to give what you have? We can all give Christ's love, God's Word, and a hug. What else have you received from God that you can share? If he has blessed you with silver and gold, are you ready to share it?

Take him by the hand
⁷ Taking him by the right hand, he helped him up, and instantly the man's feet and ankles became strong.

It was not enough for Peter to command a healing. He reached out, took his hand, and helped him up. I love the precision of God's Word: Luke records that it was his *right* hand. The lame man did not respond just to the command to rise up and walk; it was when Peter touched him that his feet and ankles became strong. Peter had to help him up. Sometimes it is not enough just to preach or say: "God bless you, brother." We have to reach out and help the person get up. Yes, it takes more time and effort. Sometimes we do not want to touch a person who is sick or dirty.

Under the law, a Jew would be made unclean. But that touch is vital. Is there someone you need to help get up? It is possible that you have preached to him and prayed for him, but he may need your hand reaching out and helping him up.

Wonder and amazement

8 He jumped up, stood on his feet, and began to walk! Then, walking, leaping, and praising God, he went into the Temple with them. (NLT)

Now, with his feet and ankles strengthened, and with Peter's help, he jumped up, as though he received an electric shock from God. For the first time in his life, he began to walk and, for the first time, entered the temple with Peter and John.

That is so important. Sometimes we minister to people on the street, but they never make it to church. Do we invite them? Would they be welcome? Some, like ex-inmates, might not be. Some might smell, or disrupt the well-planned service. Praise God for those people he has touched who jump up and praise him!

And you? When God does something beautiful in your life, do you go straight to church to give him thanks?

9 When all the people saw him walking and praising God, 10 they recognized him as the same man who used to sit begging at the temple gate called Beautiful, and they were filled with wonder and amazement at what had happened to him.

When God does a miracle like this, he loves to do it in public, for everyone to see. And he wants people to be filled with wonder and amazement! When was the last time that something happened in your life, your ministry, or your church that left people *"overcome with wonder and sheer astonishment"* (JBP)? Don't you think God would still love to glorify himself in that way?

11 While the man held on to Peter and John, all the people were astonished and came running to them in the place called Solomon's Colonnade.

He was not about to let go of Peter and John; he clung to them. How beautiful to have that relationship. When you minister to someone and God touches them, it is natural for them to hold onto you. Of course, we need boundaries to protect our families and personal lives, but that relationship is very important to a new believer.

The usual prayer has been forgotten; everyone runs to see this miracle man. Just like Pentecost, when they were all amazed, we have to take advantage of that opportunity to share God's Word.

Solomon's Colonnade ran the inside length of the wall that enclosed the outer court of the temple, with rows of 26-foot (8-meter) columns and a cedar roof. John 10:23 places Jesus walking in that Colonnade.

Jesus glorified

12 When Peter saw this, he said to them: "Fellow Israelites, why does this surprise you? Why do you stare at us as if by our own power or godliness we had made this man walk?

Jesus was an expert at using questions, and Peter starts his sermon with two questions. The first exposes the unbelief of these people gathered for prayer. Why are people surprised when God answers prayer or does a miracle? It should be common in our churches.

The second question exposes man's tendency to look at the vessel, the man or woman, instead of the source of the power. Peter immediately takes their eyes off himself, and that by someone who was only too eager to boast in the past. Why do we exalt the evangelist, apostle, or pastor who has an anointed ministry? Why do we fall into that temptation of implying that our ministry has something to do with our power or godliness?

[13] The God of Abraham, Isaac and Jacob, the God of our fathers, has glorified his servant Jesus. You handed him over to be killed, and you disowned him before Pilate, though he had decided to let him go. [14] You disowned the Holy and Righteous One and asked that a murderer be released to you. [15] You killed the author of life, but God raised him from the dead. We are witnesses of this.

Peter directed their attention to Jesus. There are three key points here:

1. Who Christ is: God's servant, whom the Father glorified. Christ is intimately connected with the same God whom Israel has always worshipped. Even though Peter did not introduce the idea of the trinity here, he called Jesus Holy and Righteous, making him equal to God. He is the author of life, which means he is the creator, another reference to his divinity.

2. Just like he did at Pentecost, he used several strong words to emphasize their guilt:
    a. They handed him over.
    b. They disowned him before Pilate (who had decided to release him).
    c. Instead they asked for a murderer to be released.
    d. They killed the author of life.

3. Despite that rejection, God did a great miracle and raised him from the dead; Peter and John are witnesses of that resurrection.

16 By faith in the name of Jesus, this man whom you see and know was made strong. It is Jesus' name and the faith that comes through him that has completely healed him, as you can all see.

The miracle was done through faith in Jesus. When he says it is Jesus' name that healed him, it is not just saying his name, but confessing your faith in everything that Jesus is. Peter said something very important: faith is not something that we have to develop; faith itself comes through Jesus. He gives us the capacity to believe in him. We repeatedly see the importance of faith in receiving a miracle. How is your faith?

Times of refreshing

17 "Now, fellow Israelites, I know that you acted in ignorance, as did your leaders. 18 But this is how God fulfilled what he had foretold through all the prophets, saying that his Messiah would suffer.

Peter blamed the Jews, but immediately offered them two examples of God's mercy, and how he can redeem our mistakes:

1. They acted in ignorance. Ignorance is no excuse for our sin, nor does it free us from its consequences, but the Law made a distinction between sins of presumption and sins of ignorance (Num. 15:27–31). Ignorance does affect our responsibility before God and how he responds to us. It was in another context, but what Jesus said in Luke 12:47–48 applies here as well: *"The servant who knows the master's will and does not get ready or does not do what the master wants will be beaten with many blows. But the one who does not know and does things deserving punishment will be beaten with few blows. From everyone who has been given much, much will be demanded; and from the one who has been entrusted with much, much more will be asked."*

2. As he often does in our lives, God redeems our mistakes and uses them for his purposes. The Messiah's death fulfilled prophecy. To save us, he had to die.

[19] Repent, then, and turn to God, so that your sins may be wiped out, that times of refreshing may come from the Lord, [20] and that he may send the Messiah, who has been appointed for you—even Jesus. [21] Heaven must receive him until the time comes for God to restore everything, as he promised long ago through his holy prophets.

These few words are full of meaning:

1. Although they acted in ignorance, their rejection of Jesus was still a great sin that somehow had to be wiped out. Praise God that our sins can be wiped out! To receive that forgiveness, they must repent and return to God. They are in God's holy temple, at the hour of prayer, but Peter says they are separated from God. Only through Christ can we approach God and find forgiveness. You can be in church and praying, yet, in ignorance, make mistakes. Do you believe your sins can be wiped out? Or are you far from God and need to repent and turn to him?

2. With that relationship restored, God can bless us with times of refreshing: *That time after time your souls may know the refreshment that comes from the presence of God* (JBP). Do you need that in your life right now? Is there some sin blocking it?

3. Jesus had just left this world, but the focus is on his return. Right now, he must stay in heaven, but at the right time, God will send him back to this earth.

4. First, there must be a restoration of all things.

5. The prophets laid out this entire plan. The message Peter gave the Jews was not new; it was the fulfillment of prophecies about the Messiah.

Jesus: the fulfillment of prophecy

22 For Moses said, 'The Lord your God will raise up for you a prophet like me from among your own people; you must listen to everything he tells you. 23 Anyone who does not listen to him will be completely cut off from their people.'

Peter appealed to Moses and pointed to Jesus as the fulfillment of the prophecy that another prophet like him would come. This is in the Old Testament Law: Anyone who would not listen to him must be destroyed. Apart from Jesus, it is impossible to be part of God's people and enter his kingdom.

24 "Indeed, beginning with Samuel, all the prophets who have spoken have foretold these days. 25 And you are heirs of the prophets and of the covenant God made with your fathers. He said to Abraham, 'Through your offspring all peoples on earth will be blessed.' 26 When God raised up his servant, he sent him first to you to bless you by turning each of you from your wicked ways."

Peter had not received the revelation about the inclusion of the Gentiles in God's plan, but he quoted God's word to Abraham that this blessing is for everyone. The Jews were the first to receive it, in accordance with Old Testament prophecy, which Jesus has fulfilled. In this short message, Peter has presented him as:

- The suffering servant (13, 18).
- The prophet like Moses (22–23).
- The king from David's line (24).
- The seed of Abraham (25–26).
- The Messiah who will come again (20–21)

- God: the Holy and Righteous Author of life (14–15).

They have the opportunity to repent and enjoy the blessings of the New Covenant.

What to do after the baptism in the Holy Spirit

What did the church do after the Spirit was poured out? What did the apostles do? They seem to have learned from their mistakes in Acts 1. They did not sit down to plan more events. They kept walking like Jesus walked, in fellowship, the teaching of the Word, and with signs and wonders. This chapter is a good example of the same pattern we observe in Christ's ministry: A miracle or healing gets the people's attention, then the Word explains what happened or teaches them how to live in God's will and experience his miracles. In everything the church does, the emphasis is on the person of Jesus Christ and a relationship with him. There is no attempt to establish a religion, an institution, or an organization.

A rhythm in Acts

We can already see a rhythm in this book:

1. The believers are united in prayer, celebrating the Lord's Supper, and fed by the teaching of the Word.
2. God works sovereignly and supernaturally to bless his people, show his power, and get the attention of unbelievers.
3. A Christ-centered message is given to call the people to repentance and salvation.

Until now, this seems like paradise; there has been nothing but blessings and growth. However, we cannot forget that we are still in the world, and have an enemy who came to steal, kill, and destroy.

5

Arrested: The Church's First Test

Acts 4:1–31

It is hard to imagine how life could get any better for the apostles. After the tragedy of Christ's crucifixion and Judas' suicide, they spent time with their resurrected Lord, saw him ascend to heaven, received the promised baptism of the Holy Spirit, and saw multitudes saved, healed, and walking in victory. That is often how it is during the first months as a Christian: God protects the young believer from the devil and gives them time to get established in their faith.

It is great to have a taste of heaven, but we are still in this world. I am sure you are aware of that enemy who wants to destroy you and the church. He had to be angry. He thought he had defeated Christ on the cross, but then Jesus rose from the dead, and now there are multitudes full of the Holy Spirit. Like father, like son—the apostles are about to experience the same opposition their Master experienced. This is the first of three attacks against the church.

Peter and John in jail

The usual 3 o'clock prayer was interrupted by a beggar leaping and praising God, claiming to be healed, and a crowd listening to

43

Peter talk about Jesus. The temple leaders cannot let that continue:

¹*The priests and the captain of the temple guard and the Sadducees came up to Peter and John while they were speaking to the people. ² They were greatly disturbed because the apostles were teaching the people, proclaiming in Jesus the resurrection of the dead. ³ They seized Peter and John and, because it was evening, they put them in jail until the next day.*

They did not even let them finish preaching. The priests, Sadducees, and captain of the temple guard must have made quite an impression as they surrounded the apostles (the Pharisees are notable in their absence). They were indignant with this spectacle, especially since it centered on the Messiah they had crucified. With his death, they thought they would be free of this problem, but things are going from bad to worse. And these men are uneducated and not approved by the religious leaders!

Their solution is to seize them and throw them in jail. Later, there were miraculous deliverances, but not this time. They would spend the night in jail and appear before the Council the next day. It does not say how they spent the night—they may have expected to be crucified, like their Lord.

⁴ *But many who heard the message believed; so the number of men who believed grew to about five thousand.*

As happens so often in the Bible and as we walk with Jesus, in the worst circumstances, God has a "but." What are you struggling with right now? How has the enemy attacked you—perhaps even through religious people? What is your "but"?

Despite the opposition, the "but" here is abundant fruit. The second chapter finished with more than three thousand believers; now there are about five thousand, and that is just the men! We are probably talking about more than ten thousand believers, and I am sure many of them were praying for Peter and John. Thank God, the church is prospering. Only the leaders are suffering, and that is often how it is: while the church enjoys God's blessings, the pastor pays the price as the target of Satan's attacks.

Peter and John before the Council

5 The next day the rulers, the elders and the teachers of the law met in Jerusalem. 6 Annas the high priest was there, and so were Caiaphas, John, Alexander and others of the high priest's family. 7 They had Peter and John brought before them and began to question them: "By what power or what name did you do this?"

It must have been intimidating to stand before all these important people. First, they want to know by what power, or through whom, they healed the man, probably trying to connect them to Jesus. There is healing in Jesus' name. There is salvation in his name. It is the name above all names. The world and the devil hate the name of Jesus. When I worked as a chaplain in the federal prisons, they asked me to pray for a graduation—but it had to be a "generic" prayer, without using Jesus' name, since various religions would be represented. I told them I could only pray in Jesus' name, and they let me pray in that wonderful, powerful name!

Jesus promised that when they were brought before the authorities, the Spirit would give them words to defend themselves (Lk. 12:12), and that is precisely what happened here. Peter was already baptized in the Spirit, but as we often see in times of need, there was a special filling of the Spirit—trust in the Lord for that filling, and the words to speak.

8 Then Peter, filled with the Holy Spirit, said to them: "Rulers and elders of the people! 9 If we are being called to account today for an act of kindness shown to a man who was lame and are being asked how he was healed, ¹⁰ then know this, you and all the people of Israel: It is by the name of Jesus Christ of Nazareth, whom you crucified but whom God raised from the dead, that this man stands before you healed. ¹¹ Jesus is

> *"'the stone you builders rejected,*
> *which has become the cornerstone.'*

¹² Salvation is found in no one else, for there is no other name under heaven given to mankind by which we must be saved."

Peter lifts up the name of Jesus! It is not Muhammad, Buddha, or anyone else. It is only Jesus. It is not being "tolerant" to say that there are many paths to God. The only way to salvation is through Jesus; every other road leads to hell. Never be shy about proclaiming Jesus' name. God will back you up. Once again, Peter blames them for Jesus' death. These leaders were the ones tasked with building God's house in Judah, but they had rejected the cornerstone, Jesus Christ. The Father raised him from the dead and made him the chief cornerstone. Is Jesus the cornerstone of your life and your church?

The case is ridiculous: They are being interrogated for an *act of kindness*, a good deed, shown to a cripple. How can they argue with that? If you get in trouble with the authorities, let it be for a good deed like this healing, and not for some foolishness! There is not much Peter can say; the case is closed, it is a simple matter of Jesus doing a miracle.

The Council's decision

¹³ When they saw the courage of Peter and John and realized that they were unschooled, ordinary men, they were astonished and they took note that these men had been with Jesus. ¹⁴ But since they could see the man who had been healed standing there with them, there was nothing they could say.

Jesus loves to confound people! Four things impress these leaders and leave them astonished:

1. The courage with which they spoke: fearless, confident, and bold. That courage is a great weapon that God gives us against the schemes of the enemy. God wants to take the fear from your heart so you can confidently speak about Jesus.

2. They were unschooled, ordinary men. Do you think you need a degree and lots of preparation for God to use you? No way! There are highly educated—and often proud—people who speak in the flesh and could not influence anyone. God loves to use humble people whom the world looks down on to do great things. Does that mean we should not study or prepare ourselves? Of course not! The ideal is the combination of humility, Biblical knowledge, good preparation, and the Spirit's anointing.

3. They recognized that they had been with Jesus. They had probably seen them with him, but I believe they could also see Jesus in them. They had spent so much time with Jesus that they were like him. What a challenge for us! To spend so much time with the Lord that others see Jesus in us and recognize that we have been with him.

4. The evidence was in front of them in the flesh: The man everyone had seen begging was with Peter and John, obviously walking and healed. By God's grace, may our testimony not only be words, but also the evidence of lives transformed by God's power.

15 So they ordered them to withdraw from the Sanhedrin and then conferred together. 16 "What are we going to do with these men?" they asked. "Everyone living in Jerusalem knows they have performed a notable sign, and we cannot deny it. 17 But to stop this thing from spreading any further among the people, we must warn them to speak no longer to anyone in this name." 18 Then they called them in again and commanded them not to speak or teach at all in the name of Jesus.

I pray that would be true for us as well! They may try to condemn us, but all they can point to is the undeniable reality of miracles done in Jesus' name. It is also a matter of public opinion. Today, it is easy to put something on Facebook or Twitter; social media has a strong influence on the decisions of business and government.

Their solution? Threaten them and order them to stop talking and teaching in Jesus' name. How would you respond to that order? Would it be enough to silence you? The devil always wants to silence us, but Christ sent us to preach and teach his word.

19 But Peter and John replied, "Which is right in God's eyes: to listen to you, or to him? You be the judges! 20 As for us, we cannot help speaking about what we have seen and heard."

Many would say: "Okay, we just won't use Jesus' name," and not mention him in their preaching, or stay silent, but go out and keep preaching like always. But Peter and John are not afraid; they boldly defy these leaders.

Doesn't the Bible command us to obey the authorities? Are there times when it is okay to break the law? When we have to choose between obeying God and obeying man, we have to obey God. He will take care of us, or, worst case, we will die as martyrs.

There is no way you can keep quiet about something as powerful and transforming as what Peter and John had seen and heard. We cannot stop talking about Jesus!

²¹ After further threats they let them go. They could not decide how to punish them, because all the people were praising God for what had happened. ²² For the man who was miraculously healed was over forty years old.

Now we learn that the man was over forty years old. Everyone had seen him, and they were amazed at Jesus' power. Just as they were afraid to touch John the Baptist because he was so popular, they dared not punish the apostles, since everyone was praising God for the miracle.

Do you believe that God can, and wants to, do something as impressive in your city?

The first recorded prayer by the young church
²³ On their release, Peter and John went back to their own people and reported all that the chief priests and the elders had said to them. ²⁴ When they heard this, they raised their voices together in prayer to God.

We have to testify, and we have to pray. They were used to praying and raising their voices. There is great power in that united prayer.

"Sovereign Lord," they said, "you made the heavens and the earth and the sea, and everything in them. ²⁵ You spoke by the Holy Spirit through the mouth of your servant, our father David:

> *"'Why do the nations rage*
> *and the peoples plot in vain?*
> *²⁶ The kings of the earth rise up*
> *and the rulers band together*

against the Lord
and against his anointed one.'

First, they recognize who their God is: He is the sovereign Lord, the Creator of everything, including these leaders who had threatened the apostles.

Then they turn to the Scriptures and a well-known Psalm. They use the Bible to interpret the situation and guide their request. It is no surprise that there would be opposition; it was prophesied.

[27] Indeed Herod and Pontius Pilate met together with the Gentiles and the people of Israel in this city to conspire against your holy servant Jesus, whom you anointed. [28] They did what your power and will had decided beforehand should happen. [29] Now, Lord, consider their threats and enable your servants to speak your word with great boldness. [30] Stretch out your hand to heal and perform signs and wonders through the name of your holy servant Jesus."

After praising God and reflecting on what happened in the light of Scripture, they finish the prayer with a request. It had nothing to do with their own comfort or personal blessings. They handed these authorities who had threatened the apostles over to God and asked for continued boldness to proclaim the Word. It is the same combination we see so often in Jesus' ministry and here in Acts: The Word, and the confirmation in healings, signs, and wonders.

The prayer was not long, but it was powerful. How does it compare with the prayers in your church or your devotional time? How much time do you spend interceding for the work of the Gospel?

31 After they prayed, the place where they were meeting was shaken. And they were all filled with the Holy Spirit and spoke the word of God boldly.

They had passed the first test. It could have put fear in their hearts and sent them back to the safety of the Upper Room. They could have thought: "It's better to worship God, listen to the Word in the safety of this room, and pray for the salvation of Jerusalem."

From what we have seen in Acts, you might think that only the apostles were evangelizing, as in this verse:

33 With great power the apostles continued to testify to the resurrection of the Lord Jesus.

The order to stop preaching about Jesus did not affect the apostles. They continued to evangelize like always, with the supernatural power of the Holy Spirit. But it was not just them; verse 31 says they **all** *spoke the word of God boldly*. How does that compare with the prayer meetings in your church?

- Do you even have one? Does most of the church show up for it?
- Does the building shake with the presence of God Almighty?
- Does everyone leave filled with the Spirit?
- Do they boldly proclaim the Word?

6

God's Economy: No Needy Persons

Acts 4:32–5:11

Here is another passage that follows the pattern we have seen in Acts:

1. An introduction describing the church.
2. An event that impacts it.
3. The result of the Spirit's move.

Introduction: Unity characterizes the church

³² All the believers were one in heart and mind.

Unity is important. Waiting for the baptism of the Spirit, they were *united* in prayer in the Upper Room. Peter and John went up to the temple *together* and were jailed *together*. In verse 24 of this chapter, they prayed *together*. Now, in a matter of weeks, thousands of people had joined them, including:

- Believers from various nations and provinces of Israel.
- Pharisees, Sadducees, and Levites.
- People generally looked down on, like prostitutes and tax collectors.

It is hard for us to stay unified, even in a small church! Can you imagine a church with thousands of members who were *"one in heart and mind"*? What program did they have that we could use to achieve that same unity?

The answer is not a program, it is:

- Being full of the Holy Spirit.
- Constantly praying.
- The presence of God's power in miracles, signs, and wonders.
- The dynamic of new people added to the church daily.

Jesus prayed for our unity the night of his arrest (Jn. 17:21–23). When he truly is the head of the church and the Spirit is moving, we will have that unity. It is beautiful to be one in heart and mind, with your spouse, and with all the brothers and sisters in church. It is possible! But we have to pray and seek that unity. Christ does not want his body divided or fighting each other.

The impact of that unity

No one claimed that any of their possessions was their own, but they shared everything they had.

NLT: *They felt that what they owned was not their own, so they shared everything they had.*

With so much love and unity, it was natural to share everything. They were so busy in prayer, worship, evangelism, service, and the teaching of the Word that those possessions simply were not important. Notice the words Luke uses: *"No one,"* and *"everything."* It was not just the wealthy or a few naturally generous brothers; the Spirit had touched every heart. And it was not just some old clothes or that extra TV—*everything they had.* However, they did not preach the elimination of private property. It is not sinful to have possessions. It says they did not "*claim*" anything as their own; their attitude was that it did not belong to them. They had given everything to Christ for him to use as he wanted.

Like everything we have seen in Acts up to this point, this is not a program. They did not have to submit a list of their possessions to "deposit" in the church's "bank." Nobody was judged because they held onto something. It was not required to give up everything to be part of the church. It was all guided by the Spirit. When we pressure the church to share everything they have, we are back under the law, and no law required us to share. It flows naturally from a heart that's grateful to God.

[33] God's grace was so powerfully at work in them all [34] that there were no needy persons among them. For from time to time those who owned land or houses sold them, brought the money from the sales [35] and put it at the apostles' feet, and it was distributed to anyone who had need.

God's grace was manifest in the elimination of financial need in the church. Nobody got rich; in fact, those who had houses or land sold them and gave the money to the church. God blesses his church through members of the body. He does not want anyone needy in his church, but they were not preaching prosperity—this was a redistribution so that everyone would be at the same level. Paul's example in the collections he received for needy churches confirms that this was not just within one local body. Rich churches in prosperous countries should share with their brothers in abject poverty. For inequality to exist is a condemnation of rich believers.

This might sound like socialism or communism, but there are some important differences:

- It was voluntary. The Bible never says it is a sin to have your own house or land.
- It did not involve every property. The church should never obligate someone to sell their house.
- It never says that selling properties or tithing was a requirement to be baptized and be part of the church.

Two examples of property sales

³⁶ Joseph, a Levite from Cyprus, whom the apostles called Barnabas (which means "son of encouragement"), ³⁷ sold a field he owned and brought the money and put it at the apostles' feet.

A brother from the priestly tribe who would play an important role in Paul's ministry is introduced here. He was a native of Cyprus, an island in the Mediterranean Sea and a destination for two of Paul's missionary journeys (the first one with this same Barnabas). The fact that Luke points out the sale of his property is evidence that not everyone sold theirs.

Judas Iscariot was the treasurer for the apostles, and he was a thief. Now, under the guidance of the Holy Spirit, the apostles are managing large amounts of money, which was literally placed at their feet. With so much money coming into the church, it would be tempting to abuse it. If we follow the early church's example, we need very definite and transparent procedures to ensure that all the money is managed in a responsible way worthy of the Lord.

The second example

Despite the Spirit's powerful presence, there was still sin in the church, which God strongly judged as a warning to the whole body: Don't play with God—or with his church.

⁵:¹ Now a man named Ananias, together with his wife Sapphira, also sold a piece of property. ² With his wife's full knowledge he kept back part of the money for himself, but brought the rest and put it at the apostles' feet.

It does not seem like a big problem. It is no sin to hold onto some of the money. In fact, it is great that they brought a large amount to place at the apostles' feet. No one was forced to hand over all the money they got from a sale. The problem lies elsewhere. Sometimes the sin is not the act itself, but the person's heart and motive.

Some husbands deceive their wives, lying about an offering made to the church and keeping part of the money for some illicit purpose, but Ananias had his wife's full cooperation.

³ Then Peter said, "Ananias, how is it that Satan has so filled your heart that you have lied to the Holy Spirit and have kept for yourself some of the money you received for the land? ⁴ Didn't it belong to you before it was sold? And after it was sold, wasn't the money at your disposal? What made you think of doing such a thing? You have not lied just to human beings but to God."

Peter confirms that there is nothing wrong with private property. Even the amount given to the church is our decision (hopefully guided by the Spirit). The problem here is the deceit and lies. They want to impress the church with their generosity and hide the truth from the apostles. It is the same hypocrisy Jesus so forcefully condemned.

Peter recognizes the source of this sin as the father of lies, the deceiver. We cannot attribute every sin to the devil, but the Spirit reveals that Satan inspired this lie. It is the first mention of the devil working in a church that until now has seemed almost perfect. He can work in a believer and even fill his heart, although many would say that this couple was not really saved. Money is problematic for many believers.

So is lying, although most Christians do not consider it a grave sin. To lie to a pastor about some ministry done in the church or about the amount of money given in an offering is fairly common. However, Revelation 21:8 includes liars among those destined for the lake of fire—along with the cowardly, the unbelieving, the vile, the murderers, the sexually immoral, those who practice magic arts, and idolaters. To lie to a church leader is to lie to the Holy Spirit dwelling in that person; they are lying to God (and in saying this, Peter affirms that the Spirit is God). Again, we see a God-given boldness in Peter, inspired by the revelation of the truth and insight into what is happening in a person's life. Do you have that boldness to confront lies and sin in your church?

How about lying? Have you lied to a pastor? Have you tried to deceive the church to impress them and appear more holy? Are you more like Barnabas or Ananias?

5 When Ananias heard this, he fell down and died. And great fear seized all who heard what had happened. 6 Then some young men came forward, wrapped up his body, and carried him out and buried him.

Just as God sternly judged sin during Israel's exodus, here, at the beginning of the church, he wants to impress them with the seriousness and the consequences of sin. With good reason, great fear seized those who heard about this. Where is that fear in the church today? How many would die if God were to judge lying and other sins in this way? Truly, the wages of sin are always death, eternally, and sometimes on earth as well. Some have said Ananias died of shock at being exposed, but I believe God killed him.

This story is similar to the tragedy of Achan in Joshua 7, during the conquest of the Promised Land. He and his family perished because of his greed and disobedience.

⁷ About three hours later his wife came in, not knowing what had happened. ⁸ Peter asked her, "Tell me, is this the price you and Ananias got for the land?"

God often gives us the chance to confess, repent, and save our lives. Instead of confronting her with her husband's sin, Peter gives her a chance to tell the truth. Sapphira was offered a way out of temptation, but she did not take it.

"Yes," she said, "that is the price." ⁹ Peter said to her, "How could you conspire to test the Spirit of the Lord? Listen! The feet of the men who buried your husband are at the door, and they will carry you out also." ¹⁰ At that moment she fell down at his feet and died. Then the young men came in and, finding her dead, carried her out and buried her beside her husband.

Earlier, Peter said Ananias *lied* to the Spirit; now, he says they conspired *to test the Spirit of the Lord*. Could God be giving you an opportunity, as Peter gave Sapphira, to confess sin and repent?

Once again, some have said that the shock of her husband's death killed her, but I believe God killed her.

The result
¹¹ Great fear seized the whole church and all who heard about these events.

Yes, there were miracles, joy, love, and changed lives in the early church. Praise God! But now there is a powerful reminder that God is holy. He is the same God of the Old Testament who cannot tolerate sin—he wants his Son's body to be pure and spotless. He is patient and merciful, but there is also a coming judgment. Great fear seized the whole church, and also in the surrounding community.

Is it possible to live the economy of the early church today?

Just as many try to minimize Jesus' teachings (and the Bible in general), many scholars and pastors say that this economy was only for that time; we cannot experience it today. Indeed, it is not presented as a model for every church in every age, even though Jesus taught many similar, radical things about money and material things (read chapters 16–18 in the second book in this series, Kingdom Culture).

Through the centuries, there have been many attempts to follow this model, in monasteries and Christian communities. Most of them have failed, often with abusive and even criminal activity. Money presents us with many temptations, including the sin of Ananias and Sapphira. The Bible teaches that it is hard for the rich to faithfully follow Christ—the poor person who has nothing to sell is exempt from this couple's sin.

Some important principles in this passage for your reflection:

1. This economy was the direct result of the fullness and work of the Holy Spirit in the church. We cannot organize it and direct it; it has to be the Spirit's work, or it will fail.
2. We need transparency and clear procedures in how we manage offerings, doing everything possible to avoid abuses with money in the church.
3. God wants equality among his children. The biblical pattern is for those with more resources to share with those who have few: *There need be no poor people among you, for in the land the Lord your God is giving you to possess as your inheritance, he will richly bless you* (Deut. 15:4).

4. We need to evaluate the current tendency to preach prosperity and approve of the world's materialism and greed.

5. The Spirit might guide you to sell a property or something else to give as an offering to the church.

6. We must always avoid hypocrisy and the carnal desire to impress others with our spirituality.

7. It is too common and too easy to overlook sin in the church, such as the sin of Ananias and Sapphira. God may sovereignly discipline someone, but we need leaders like Peter, with spiritual discernment, and procedures for discipline in the church. Too many pastors will receive any offering without question, even if it might be stolen or dirty money.

8. We have already seen this sharing of resources twice in the book of Acts:

   a. 2:44–45: *All the believers were together and had everything in common. They sold property and possessions to give to anyone who had need.*

   b. 4:34–35: *There were no needy persons among them. For from time to time those who owned land or houses sold them, brought the money from the sales and put it at the apostles' feet, and it was distributed to anyone who had need.*

   The repetition points to its prevalence and importance.

7

A Miraculous Jail Break

Acts 5:12–42

We have noted a pattern in this book: an event, a miracle or sermon, and then an update of the current status of the church. The first opposition from the religious establishment—the arrest of Peter and John after the healing of the cripple in chapter 4—did not stop the church's growth. When a serious sin was committed by church members, the Lord got rid of the sinners and, sobered, the church moved forward.

You can see a similar pattern in Jesus' life, and you may experience it when you walk like Jesus walked. It could start with an unexpected illness, accident, family problem, or economic crisis. At first, it seems like a disaster—you may be confused and ask God "why"? However, the Lord helps you, and his hand is evident. You end up at peace and stronger than before.

A supernatural life
This portion starts with a rather lengthy update on the church's status:

12 The apostles performed many signs and wonders among the people. And all the believers used to meet together in Solomon's Colonnade.

It is a supernatural atmosphere, following the pattern of Jesus' ministry: signs and wonders preparing people for the word, which has already won thousands for the kingdom—here only signs and wonders are mentioned.

What is impressive is the corporate life of the church and their daily meetings in the temple, in Solomon's Colonnade, where Peter preached in chapter 3. *All* the believers gathered there. Rarely would we find *all* the believers in a church present for a service, but here the Lord moved so powerfully that nobody wanted to miss a meeting, and they were *all in one accord* (NASB). Despite the large number of new believers and their diversity, they maintained their unity.

13 No one else dared join them, even though they were highly regarded by the people. 14 Nevertheless, more and more men and women believed in the Lord and were added to their number.

How strange. Multitudes joined the church, but it says that no one else dared join them. Luke is probably referring to Jews who had not accepted Jesus; he is making an obvious distinction between believers and unbelievers. Fear or awe has been mentioned several times, and perhaps the experience of Ananias and Sapphira added to it. Nevertheless, somehow, many overcame it to trust in Jesus and join the church.

How wonderful that the believers maintained an outstanding testimony in their daily lives and were highly regarded and respected by the whole community. Their lives and example attracted the unbelievers and resulted in many conversions. Isn't that the church Jesus wants? Isn't it what you want in a church?

Fellowship, unity, supernatural manifestations of God's power, and a good reputation with the community. Do you believe it is possible today? It should be the norm.

15 As a result, people brought the sick into the streets and laid them on beds and mats so that at least Peter's shadow might fall on some of them as he passed by.

This is impacting the entire city. Peter has become a superstar of sorts, with such a high reputation and so much anointing and spiritual power that his very shadow falling on someone can heal them.

16 Crowds gathered also from the towns around Jerusalem, bringing their sick and those tormented by impure spirits, and all of them were healed.

Here are two words already seen many times in Acts: "crowds" and "everyone," or "all." No wonder there were crowds! There is great faith and expectation! They brought in the sick and tormented from all the neighboring towns, and everyone was healed. It is similar to stories of a revival impacting an entire country. It is a transformation. Everyone is talking about this Jesus who continues to work miracles through his disciples.

The Devil Says "Enough:" The Apostles Put in Jail
Sadly, when God moves with so much power, other pastors and churches may be envious; in this case, it was the priests and Jewish leaders. What can they do? They have already threatened Peter and John, but that only emboldened them. We know that our fight is not against flesh and blood (Eph. 6:12), but against the principalities and powers of the evil one. This is the second of three attempts by the religious establishment to stop the church.

17 Then the high priest and all his associates, who were members of the party of the Sadducees, were filled with jealousy. 18 They arrested the apostles and put them in the public jail.

This is also the second time they were imprisoned. It does not say exactly who they were; surely Peter and John, but possibly all the apostles.

God provides another "but"

19 But during the night an angel of the Lord opened the doors of the jail and brought them out. 20 "Go, stand in the temple courts," he said, "and tell the people all about this new life."

The Bible is full of "buts," and this "but" is powerful. No one asked for it or declared it. God acted sovereignly. A prison is no problem for God; he just sends an angel to open the doors and get you out of jail. Many prisoners have asked God to send that angel to their jail! We know that God can do it—praise him for those miracles! However, as we saw in chapter 4, we also know that it is not always the case.

So what does the angel command them to do after opening the prison doors? Forget about hiding, leaving Jerusalem for a quieter place, or at least not preaching publicly in the temple. They are to go right back to the temple courts and continue preaching.

What would you do? Are you obedient to share the message of new life despite the consequences?

21 At daybreak they entered the temple courts, as they had been told, and began to teach the people. When the high priest and his associates arrived, they called together the Sanhedrin—the full assembly of the elders of Israel—and sent to the jail for the apostles. 22 But on arriving at the jail, the officers did not find them there. So they went back and reported, 23 "We found the jail securely locked, with the guards standing at the doors; but when we opened them, we found no one inside."

Three different scenarios at dawn:
1. In the temple, the apostles began to teach. They did not even wait one hour to minister to people. There was no evidence of fear; they obeyed the Lord's word.
2. In the great hall of the general assembly, the elders of Israel, led by the high priest, convened the Council (the Sanhedrin), hoping to stop this movement. Whether it is crucifixion or prison, they must do something to maintain their position and the peace of Jerusalem.
3. The jail was empty, but there was no evidence of an escape. Everything was in order—the angel closed the doors after taking them out!—but there was a big surprise inside. The guards brought the news to the Council.

[24] On hearing this report, the captain of the temple guard and the chief priests were at a loss, wondering what this might lead to. [25] Then someone came and said, "Look! The men you put in jail are standing in the temple courts teaching the people." [26] At that, the captain went with his officers and brought the apostles. They did not use force, because they feared that the people would stone them.

It is great when God's work leaves your enemies perplexed. There was no explanation for the apostles' presence in the temple, and they already had a large audience at that early hour—so many that the guards feared being stoned by them. The apostles did not resist; they knew they were in God's will and trusted in him, no matter what might happen.

The apostles before the Council

²⁷ The apostles were brought in and made to appear before the Sanhedrin to be questioned by the high priest. ²⁸ "We gave you strict orders not to teach in this name," he said. "Yet you have filled Jerusalem with your teaching and are determined to make us guilty of this man's blood."

The root of their anger was guilt over Jesus' death. It is Jesus' name that is always the problem. We have to teach and minister in that name, as if Jesus himself were speaking. When we do, his power is released. This is not "evangelistic exaggeration" (which, sadly, many ministers commit). The truth is that the city was full of this teaching; everyone talked about the church and the miracles.

How will the apostles respond? What would you say?

²⁹ Peter and the other apostles replied: "We must obey God rather than human beings!

Peter already told them the same thing last time. It is a delicate subject, because the Bible also teaches the importance of obeying the God-ordained authorities. However, when there is a clear conflict between God's will and that of unconverted men, we have to obey God, despite the consequences. Just be sure that God has commanded it, and it is not just an excuse to do what you want to do.

³⁰ The God of our ancestors raised Jesus from the dead—whom you killed by hanging him on a cross. ³¹ God exalted him to his own right hand as Prince and Savior that he might bring Israel to repentance and forgive their sins. ³² We are witnesses of these things, and so is the Holy Spirit, whom God has given to those who obey him."

Given the circumstances, you might expect Peter to say something to calm the Council, but he strongly accused them of being responsible for the death of the "Prince and Savior." Again, Jesus is the focus of his short message. The apostles were witnesses of the risen Christ and could not stop sharing this good news of repentance and forgiveness of sins that Israel so badly needs. And they are not the only ones; the Holy Spirit is also a witness.

Peter said something interesting about the baptism in the Spirit here: it is a gift, but not for everyone. It is for those who *obey* God. This same Spirit works with us today to testify about Jesus Christ. Peter began and ended speaking about obedience. Were these Jewish leaders obedient to God? Peter did not say it, but it is obvious he believed they were not. The apostles have experienced the blessings of obedience, especially the presence of the Holy Spirit, and they were not going to risk that anointing by disobeying their Lord.

And you? How is your obedience? If you no longer experience the fullness of the Spirit, could disobedience be the cause?

The Council's decision
33 When they heard this, they were furious and wanted to put them to death.

It was infuriating!

- They crucified Jesus to end his teachings, but God raised him up.
- They commanded the apostles not to speak in Jesus' name, but the popular support and evidence of all the healings and deliverances is so great that they were afraid to kill them.

- They arrested and imprisoned them, but an angel opened the prison doors.

These were poor, uneducated, ordinary men versus the Council of the best-educated, wealthiest, most powerful men in Judah. And they were powerless against the apostles! Peter did nothing to accommodate or reassure them. The only solution seems to be to kill them, but God had plans for them, and he raised up an unexpected defender:

[34] But a Pharisee named Gamaliel, a teacher of the law, who was honored by all the people, stood up in the Sanhedrin and ordered that the men be put outside for a little while. [35] Then he addressed the Sanhedrin: "Men of Israel, consider carefully what you intend to do to these men. [36] Some time ago Theudas appeared, claiming to be somebody, and about four hundred men rallied to him. He was killed, all his followers were dispersed, and it all came to nothing. [37] After him, Judas the Galilean appeared in the days of the census and led a band of people in revolt. He too was killed, and all his followers were scattered. [38] Therefore, in the present case I advise you: Leave these men alone! Let them go! For if their purpose or activity is of human origin, it will fail. [39] But if it is from God, you will not be able to stop these men; you will only find yourselves fighting against God."

In these situations, it is easy to respond with emotion, and especially anger. Few people analyze the situation, reflect on history and what has happened in other similar situations, and speak wisely. I believe God inspired Gamaliel to say these words.

There are times in scripture when we have to remind ourselves that some words are from people who do not know God. Gamaliel's words are cited many times as a guarantee that something of human origin will fail and something of God cannot be destroyed. It may be true in many cases, but we also know that many things of human origin have prospered, and there are works of God that evil men have destroyed. It is hard to fight against God, but many do.

Possibly, Gamaliel had heard Jesus' teachings and had true faith in God. He was the grandson of the famous Rabbi Hillel, was Saul's teacher, and was highly respected by all the people. Indeed, his words express that faith: leave the apostles in God's hands.

40 His speech persuaded them. They called the apostles in and had them flogged. Then they ordered them not to speak in the name of Jesus, and let them go.

They accepted what Gamaliel said and released them, but not before whipping them and ordering them not to speak in Jesus' name.

They don't stop walking with Jesus

41 The apostles left the Sanhedrin, rejoicing because they had been counted worthy of suffering disgrace for the Name. 42 Day after day, in the temple courts and from house to house, they never stopped teaching and proclaiming the good news that Jesus is the Messiah.

Just like the first time the apostles were threatened (in chapter 4), this only served to encourage them. They cannot stop teaching and announcing the good news; every day they are ministering, not only in the temple, but also from house to house. Again, the passage ends with the church victorious.

A Pause

Let's take a break here to catch our breath. We do not know precisely how much time has passed in these first five chapters of Acts, but it has been spectacular. It is like being in heaven. God allowed it to establish his church. Unfortunately, we are still on this earth, and this taste of heaven, this honeymoon, will soon be over.

It is worth reflecting on the most important things we have seen in these chapters:

The transforming work of the Holy Spirit. Even more than physically being in Jesus' presence, the baptism of the Spirit transformed a man like Peter: from an impulsive man who even denied Jesus, to the leader of the young church with the courage to preach, confront the authorities, and minister with so much power that people wanted his shadow to fall on them.

An abundance of miracles. It says that *all* the sick were healed and *all* the tormented were delivered. It is the continuation of Jesus' ministry and the fulfillment of his promise that they would do the same works—and even greater.

God's sovereignty. The apostles did not plan Pentecost; it was a sovereign move of God. When the apostles were imprisoned, an angel released them.

Massive conversions. Thousands accepted Jesus in this short time. Acts repeatedly talks about the growth of the church. Although our focus is not on numbers—the quality of believers is more important than their quantity—it is obvious that the normal course of a Spirit-filled church is remarkable growth.

The power of biblical, anointed, Christ-centered preaching. There is no manipulation of people or long messages. They are not afraid to talk about sin and the need for repentance. They do not entertain or tell stories of their personal experiences with Jesus. They quote the Bible and talk about who Jesus is.

Genuine fellowship and evident love among believers. They want to be together, every day, in the temple and in homes. They share the Lord's Supper to remind themselves that Jesus is the reason for their existence. There is impressive unity.

They enjoy everyone's favor and respect. There is no evidence of hypocrisy or anything that would harm the church's reputation. God dealt swiftly with the one exception, Ananias and Sapphira.

They share their assets and money. The manifestation of Christ's love eliminates all need in the church.

There is a healthy fear of God. The deaths of Ananias and Sapphira confirm that God takes holiness and honesty in his church seriously.

A word that sums up these chapters is "supernatural." It is an experience totally out of the ordinary for this world.

Was it unique? Many scholars say: "Yes." God worked in a very special way to establish the church, but today it is impossible to have the same experience.

I say: "Why not?" Jesus never said that our experience would cease to be supernatural. He gave the expectation of greater works and the amazing baptism of the Holy Spirit. I long for what I see in these chapters, and I believe every sincere Christian does. Of course, there are seasons in our lives and in the church. It is beneficial to study the history of the church through the centuries.

If you ever have doubts about God and the Bible, these chapters should eliminate them. This is pure history. There is no doubt that these people existed and that the church was established during that time in Jerusalem. Some may dispute the stories of Eden or the great flood, but something powerful happened in these years that established the Christian church as the world's dominant religion, which has transformed millions of lives. We are in direct line with Peter and the other apostles, and we still experience the same baptism in the Holy Spirit.

8

A Threat to the Church's Unity and its Resolution

Acts 6:1–7:70

¹In those days when the number of disciples was increasing, the Hellenistic Jews among them complained against the Hebraic Jews because their widows were being overlooked in the daily distribution of food.

The problem

The church's experience of heaven had been shattered from without by attacks from the religious authorities, and from within by the lies and deaths of Ananias and Sapphira. The devil had tried to corrupt the church, but God moved swiftly to preserve its purity. Now there was a more serious problem from within that had the potential to divide the church.

The apostles did not respond to the church's growth with programs, and we have no record of Jesus talking about a feeding program for widows. Jesus commanded us to make disciples, heal the sick, deliver the demonized, and love others. However, love manifests itself in daily life and in caring for those in need, and it almost always touches our wallets in some way. Of their own free will, the brothers sold houses and land, handing the money over to the apostles and impressively eliminating all financial need in the church. They also established a daily food distribution for the widows, which could have been massive in a church of more than 10,000 people. Such an extensive program invites abuse and complaints. Despite God's presence in the church, they were still human, and there was a problem.

There will always be problems, and, unfortunately, there will always be complaints, even among Spirit-filled believers. Grumbling and complaining were a fatal problem for the Hebrews on the exodus, and now the church had been invaded by them. When the devil does not achieve his ends with attacks from without, he can use gossip and complaints to destroy it from within.

Problems of race, culture, nationality, and language are not new. Those natural divisions test the unity of any church, even the early church. Some of the believers spoke Greek. They were raised in other provinces of the empire, the result of the Jewish Diaspora, and had a very different culture from the Aramaic-speaking Jews in Judah. The language difference creates difficulties, plus the Greek-speakers tended to be more prosperous and better educated. However, they were "foreigners," and somehow—whether real or perceived is unclear—they felt their widows were overlooked (NLT: *discriminated against*) in the food distribution. The sad reality is that discrimination is all too common in the church today, whether based on race, language, culture, class, or any other difference. We must watch for and fight that discrimination.

The solution

²So the Twelve gathered all the disciples together and said, "It would not be right for us to neglect the ministry of the word of God in order to wait on tables. ³Brothers and sisters, choose seven men from among you who are known to be full of the Spirit and wisdom. We will turn this responsibility over to them ⁴and will give our attention to prayer and the ministry of the word."

The Twelve took the initiative: They did not act in secret, but brought the entire community together and presented a solution. Apparently, it was a matter of priorities and time: the apostles not only preached and ministered, but they also managed these programs. Many pastors need to prioritize prayer and the ministry of the word over managing details of buildings and programs.

Their solution was to delegate and entrust faithful men with carefully serving and caring for all the widows. Instead of choosing them, the apostles trusted the church to make the selection, giving them ownership of the program. The apostles only required the seven candidates (the biblical number of completion) to meet these qualifications:

1. Men—and they were men—of good reputation.
2. Spirit-filled men.
3. Men full of wisdom.

It was not about ability, but character and spirituality. The qualifications for a ministry of service are as high as for the ministry of the Word. Sometimes a church chooses someone highly educated or successful in business who seems qualified as an administrator, but lacks the necessary spiritual qualifications. Do you look for these qualities in deacons in your church? Do you even have deacons?

⁵ This proposal pleased the whole group. They chose Stephen, a man full of faith and of the Holy Spirit; also Philip, Procorus, Nicanor, Timon, Parmenas, and Nicolas from Antioch, a convert to Judaism. ⁶ They presented these men to the apostles, who prayed and laid their hands on them.

When the Spirit inspires us with a wise plan, it will please the whole church. It does not say how they were chosen (not by casting lots!), but they were presented to the apostles, who did not question their choice, but prayed and laid hands on them to ordain them to this ministry.

They all had Greek names, implying that even the Aramaic-speaking deacons had knowledge of Greek culture. From the beginning, Stephen (who was named first) was distinguished as a man full of faith and the Spirit. Of the others, we will meet Philip in chapter 8, and Nicholas was a proselyte—a gentile who had accepted the Jewish religion—from the city of Antioch, and therefore Greek-speaking. The group had the necessary diversity to serve the Greek widows well.

The result

⁷ So the word of God spread. The number of disciples in Jerusalem increased rapidly, and a large number of priests became obedient to the faith.

This verse follows the typical pattern of Acts, with an update on the state of the church. This is the first of six summaries of church growth in Acts (9:31, 12:24, 16:5, 19:20, and 28:30–31). The message is clear: The nature of the church is to grow.

The apostles, freed from the details of the feeding program, dedicated themselves to the Word, which spread even more. When we do things in obedience to the Spirit, we will see more growth. Even many priests accepted Jesus as their Messiah, and the number of disciples increased rapidly. That success and growth often lead to envy and persecution.

Opposition due to jealousy

⁸ Now Stephen, a man full of God's grace and power, performed great wonders and signs among the people.

Have you noticed the importance of men walking with Jesus in the power of the Spirit? So far in Acts, Peter has stood out, but God is already raising others up. Unfortunately, Stephen's powerful ministry will be short-lived, but we will soon see Philip, Paul, Barnabas, and others who are instruments in the Lord's hands. Could you be a man or woman that God uses in signs and wonders?

Stephen was selected to work with the feeding ministry, but he clearly had a broader calling. That often happens in church: someone starts with a humble ministry, but, as he serves faithfully, God opens other doors. We already know that Stephen was full of the Spirit, faith, and wisdom, and had a good reputation; now it says he was filled with God's grace and power.

⁹ Then some of those who belonged to the synagogue of the Freedmen (as it was called), and of the Cyrenians, and of the Alexandrians, and of those from Cilicia and Asia, rose up and disputed with Stephen. (ESV)

We know there was tension between Aramaic-speaking and Greek-speaking believers. Just as we do today, the Jews had synagogues made up mainly of one ethnic group. There are two minority groups named here:

1. A synagogue made up of freed slaves and their descendants.

2. A group of foreigners; Jews by birth and some proselytes, but from different cultures.

We do not know why they argued with Stephen; it may have had something to do with the feeding of the widows, but more likely it was the power of his ministry of word and miraculous signs that drew many from those groups to Christ.

10 But they could not stand up against the wisdom the Spirit gave him as he spoke. 11 Then they secretly persuaded some men to say, "We have heard Stephen speak blasphemous words against Moses and against God."

The evil person becomes even more frustrated when he cannot stand up against the Christian. The Holy Spirit inspired Stephen, and they could not compete with his wisdom, so they made up a very serious case, of blasphemy against Moses and God. The devil used them to instigate others, and, sadly, many believed the lies. Do the accusations against Stephen sound familiar? They said the same thing about Jesus (Mark 14:64, John 10:33).

We must be cautious with what we believe on social networks. Everyone has opinions and complaints. Theological arguments are always dangerous, and can quickly descend into slander, lies, and even legal action. Resist the temptation to fall into them.

Stephen before the Council

12 So they stirred up the people and the elders and the teachers of the law. They seized Stephen and brought him before the Sanhedrin. 13 They produced false witnesses, who testified, "This fellow never stops speaking against this holy place and against the law. 14 For we have heard him say that this Jesus of Nazareth will destroy this place and change the customs Moses handed down to us."

These are not the Jewish leaders stirring up the people; they are from a foreigners' synagogue, but a few people can cause chaos. With so many people involved, they easily seized Stephen and brought him before the Sanhedrin (the Council of the Jewish leaders). Just as with Jesus, the lies made a fair trial impossible. Interestingly, their accusations focus on a building (the temple) and traditions that were not actually part of the law. This is the third (and strongest) of the devil's attempts to destroy the church.

Was there any basis for their accusations? Jesus indeed said that his spiritual body, the church, would take the place of the temple, and Jerusalem would no longer be the center of worship. Jesus also prophesied, correctly, that the temple would be destroyed, as it was in 70 AD by the Romans, and was never rebuilt. Jesus frequently spoke against the traditions the Jews had added to the law, most notably in the Sermon on the Mount. Jesus himself is the fulfillment of the law.

[15] *All who were sitting in the Sanhedrin looked intently at Stephen, and they saw that his face was like the face of an angel.*

They could not stop looking at Stephen's face; they had never seen anyone so angelic.

Stephen's sermon

Chapter six is the shortest in Acts; chapter seven is the longest. Most of it is Stephen's message to the Sanhedrin. It begins by summarizing the history of Israel in four periods:

1. Abraham and the patriarchs (7:2–8).
2. Joseph and the exile in Egypt (9–19).
3. Moses and the exodus in the wilderness (20–44), where their hard hearts were exposed by their rebellion and desire to return to Egypt.
4. David and Solomon, and the establishment of the monarchy (45–50).

During each of those periods, God's presence was not limited to one place. He is a living god, who moves and does new things. The Most High does not live in houses built by human hands (7:48). Thus, Stephen downplayed the importance they gave to the temple—and should make us question our attraction to buildings.

They listened carefully up to that point, but Stephen condemns them, undoubtedly aware of what their reaction would be:

[51] *"You stiff-necked people! Your hearts and ears are still uncircumcised. You are just like your ancestors: You always resist the Holy Spirit!* [52] *Was there ever a prophet your ancestors did not persecute? They even killed those who predicted the coming of the Righteous One. And now you have betrayed and murdered him—* [53] *you who have received the law that was given through angels but have not obeyed it."*

This is a brave, fearless man, despite knowing he will probably be killed. Again and again, he denounces them:

- They are stubborn.
- Hard of heart.
- Their ears are uncircumcised.
- Like their ancestors, they always resist the Holy Spirit.
- Like them, they persecute God's prophets.
- They killed John the Baptist, who announced the coming of the Messiah.
- They betrayed and murdered Jesus, the Righteous One.

They had the great privilege of receiving the law given by angels, the same law Stephen's accusers say he speaks against, but they have not obeyed it! With that condemnation, what other option do his accusers have?

The first martyr

54 When the members of the Sanhedrin heard this, they were furious and gnashed their teeth at him. 55 But Stephen, full of the Holy Spirit, looked up to heaven and saw the glory of God, and Jesus standing at the right hand of God. 56 "Look," he said, "I see heaven open and the Son of Man standing at the right hand of God."

The stones did not bother Stephen; he had already seen Jesus and the glory of heaven! We think of Christ sitting at the right hand of the Father, but here he is standing, perhaps ready to receive Stephen.

57 At this they covered their ears and, yelling at the top of their voices, they all rushed at him, 58 dragged him out of the city and began to stone him. Meanwhile, the witnesses laid their coats at the feet of a young man named Saul.

Meet Saul, introduced here for the first time in the Bible. Perhaps he was part of the group of foreigners, since he was from Tarsus and Greek-speaking. Although he did not participate in the stoning, the first verse of chapter eight (NLT) says: *Saul was one of the witnesses, and he agreed completely with the killing of Stephen* (why did someone separate that verse from chapter seven?). It is almost like Saul was supervising his death.

It is hard to accept change and admit being wrong. Unfortunately, throughout the centuries of church history, many people have died at the hands of other Christians who did not want to accept change or surrender their position, and did not want to admit that they were wrong or in sin.

59 While they were stoning him, Stephen prayed, "Lord Jesus, receive my spirit." 60 Then he fell on his knees and cried out, "Lord, do not hold this sin against them." When he had said this, he fell asleep.

Like Jesus, he asked forgiveness for his murderers as he died, becoming the first Christian martyr. Why would God allow someone so gifted and godly to die like this? Those are difficult questions to answer, but that day a powerful work began in the life of the young Saul, and the persecution that followed resulted in tremendous growth for the church.

9

God is Looking for Available Servants

Acts 8

Act one of this tremendous story of Acts has been in Jerusalem. This chapter, "Act 2," is a significant scene change. There were three unsuccessful attempts to silence the church, but, as always, God redeems what the devil intends for evil. Now they move beyond Jerusalem and keep expanding until the Gospel reaches the capital of the empire, Rome itself. It all begins with the hardest trial yet for the church.

The first persecution

Things can change quickly. When God moves, the devil will fight back. Do you think persecution is possible in your country? Jesus said it would be part of the last days before his coming (Jn. 16), but when there is so much blessing, it is easy to believe it does not apply to us.

The death of someone as godly as Stephen was a severe blow to the young church, but now there was an even worse threat: that Pharisee named Saul.

¹On that day a great persecution broke out against the church in Jerusalem, and all except the apostles were scattered throughout

Judea and Samaria. ² Godly men buried Stephen and mourned deeply for him. ³ But Saul began to destroy the church. Going from house to house, he dragged off both men and women and put them in prison.

This man was determined to destroy the church. No one could imagine Saul becoming Paul, one of the greatest apostles in all of history, but God can transform anyone.

The truth is that the church was very prosperous and comfortable. It would be easy to forget that just before his ascension Jesus shared the purpose of the Spirit's coming: *you will receive power when the Holy Spirit comes on you; and you will be my witnesses in Jerusalem, and in all Judea and Samaria, and to the ends of the earth* (Acts 1:8). God allowed persecution to remind them of that missionary vision and help them obey his command, scattering them to Judea and Samaria. It is better not to wait for a persecution that forces you to go to the mission field!

Philip evangelizes Samaria

Philip, described as full of the Spirit and wisdom when chosen as a deacon in chapter 6, gives us an example of how to evangelize a city and an individual, and how powerfully God can use someone available.

⁴ Those who had been scattered preached the word wherever they went. ⁵ Philip went down to a city in Samaria and proclaimed the Messiah there.

Now everyone was preaching, not just the apostles or deacons. You do not even have to be sent out as a missionary; just preach the word wherever you go.

A close friend of Stephen's, Philip left Jerusalem heavy-hearted and was still in mourning when he arrived in Samaria. It is not the first time that the gospel reached them; Jesus himself ministered there after his encounter with the Samaritan woman (Jn. 4). But, until now, no one from the church wanted to go there.

⁶ When the crowds heard Philip and saw the signs he performed, they all paid close attention to what he said. ⁷ For with shrieks, impure spirits came out of many, and many who were paralyzed or lame were healed. ⁸ So there was great joy in that city.

Once again, we see that potent combination of word and miracles. It is important to "hear" and also "see" to have faith. When the paralytics walk and the demonized are set free, everyone pays attention. That city was transformed and filled with joy. Don't you think the Lord still wants to glorify himself that way?

A complicated man

⁹ Now for some time a man named Simon had practiced sorcery in the city and amazed all the people of Samaria. He boasted that he was someone great, ¹⁰ and all the people, both high and low, gave him their attention and exclaimed, "This man is rightly called the Great Power of God."

Now there was a clash of kingdoms. Who will win? Many times in ministry, we encounter a complicated person. Until Philip's arrival, Simon was the superstar in Samaria, claiming to be someone great. Like Philip, who attracted the whole city, everyone had paid attention to Simon. He was a sorcerer, and he amazed and deceived people with his diabolical power. This would be a hard case.

¹¹ They followed him because he had amazed them for a long time with his sorcery. ¹² But when they believed Philip as he proclaimed the good news of the kingdom of God and the name of Jesus Christ, they were baptized, both men and women. ¹³ Simon himself believed and was baptized. And he followed Philip everywhere, astonished by the great signs and miracles he saw.

We already know that Philip was full of the Holy Spirit and wisdom. Despite being a deacon for a very short time, he did everything right:

- Announced the good news of the kingdom of God and the name of Jesus Christ.
- Baptized new believers.
- Did great signs and miracles.

Now his ministry would be tested. Simon already had a long history in that city and was amazed by what Philip did. He wanted to experience God's power and do signs and miracles too! But had he really repented? At this point, it is hard to know. He may have sensed that he had already lost his audience, and it would be better to join this new movement. He had been a leader with his magical arts; it was natural for him to want to be a leader in the church, so he followed Philip everywhere, and Philip allowed it. It could be a good opportunity to disciple him; Simon might be the first pastor of this new church.

There are people interested in spiritual things who, possibly in ignorance, accept doctrines of demons. There is satanic power in magic. You have to be very careful with it; Simon was accustomed to deceiving people. Philip needs great wisdom to deal with him.

Baptized in the Spirit

Apparently, the apostles had not sent Philip to Samaria, and it was a long time before the news reached Jerusalem that they had received the word of God. Despite Jesus' command to go there, the traditional Jewish prejudice against the Samaritans left the apostles doubtful about the authenticity of Philip's work, so they sent two leading apostles to investigate:

¹⁴ When the apostles in Jerusalem heard that Samaria had accepted the word of God, they sent Peter and John to Samaria. ¹⁵ When they arrived, they prayed for the new believers there that they might receive the Holy Spirit, ¹⁶ because the Holy Spirit had not yet come on any of them; they had simply been baptized in the name of the Lord Jesus. ¹⁷ Then Peter and John placed their hands on them, and they received the Holy Spirit.

How strange. Philip was filled with the Spirit, the Holy Spirit had performed great miracles, and many received the message and were baptized in water, which on other occasions included the baptism in the Spirit. However, none of the Samaritans had received the Spirit. Some scholars have suggested that God allowed it so the apostles could confirm that they were really saved. What happened is very instructive for us:

- The first thing the apostles did when they arrived was to pray for them to receive the Spirit.

- Somehow, it was obvious to them that they were not baptized in the Spirit. In their experience, when someone accepted Jesus and was baptized in water, the Spirit would descend with manifestations of tongues, just as in the upper room and when Peter preached (Acts 2:38).

- There are some sects (the most common are called "Apostolics") who do not believe in the Trinity, and say you must be baptized "in the name of Jesus only." But that was precisely the reason given here for not receiving the Spirit: they were not baptized as Jesus had commanded, in the name of the Father, the Son, and the Holy Spirit. Perhaps Philip never received instruction on how to baptize new believers.

- It appears that either everyone or no one would receive the baptism. At Pentecost, everyone was baptized. Here, the Spirit had not yet descended on *anyone*; now *everyone* received the Spirit.

- They received it when Peter and John laid hands on them.

Acts does not record the same experience each time people are baptized in the Spirit. It could be at the time of conversion, with water baptism, or a unique experience later. The essential thing is to receive it. How about you? Has the Spirit descended on you? Is making sure that people have received the Spirit an important part of your ministry?

Simon asks for the same power to minister the baptism

[18] *When Simon saw that the Spirit was given at the laying on of the apostles' hands, he offered them money* [19] *and said, "Give me also this ability so that everyone on whom I lay my hands may receive the Holy Spirit."*

There was something obvious and impressive that happened with the laying on of hands, and Simon wanted that power. He may have been sincere and was just unaware that you cannot buy the gift. Simon seems to be someone you do not want to offend. Maybe he just needed more time in discipleship, but God allowed Peter to see his heart, and he confronted him with a word of knowledge:

[20] *Peter answered: "May your money perish with you, because you thought you could buy the gift of God with money!* [21] *You have no part or share in this ministry, because your heart is not right before God.* [22] *Repent of this wickedness and pray to the*

Lord in the hope that he may forgive you for having such a thought in your heart. ²³ For I see that you are full of bitterness and captive to sin."

You cannot buy the gift of God or a position in the church. Even a seminary degree does not qualify you to administer the gift of God—you must be right before God and called by the Lord.

Peter does not assure Simon of God's forgiveness for his sin; he says the Lord may (or may not) forgive him (NLT: *Perhaps he will forgive your evil thoughts*). Simon believed, was baptized, and was close to Philip, but there was no genuine repentance. Possibly, he needed deliverance from the unclean spirits associated with his practice of the magical arts. Despite the appearances, he was still a slave to sin and full of bitterness.

²⁴ Then Simon answered, "Pray to the Lord for me so that nothing you have said may happen to me."

Someone faced with their sin and its consequences often appears repentant. We do not know if Peter prayed for him or cast out his demons; the early church fathers wrote that Simon was a heretic.

It is possible to have faith and even be baptized, and not be saved. And you? Are you really saved and free from your slavery to sin? It says that Simon was amazed by the signs and miracles he saw. Some people who come to church are amazed by God's presence, the good music, the love, and the miracles that may happen. They want to be part of it, but they have not repented and are not saved.

²⁵ After they had further proclaimed the word of the Lord and testified about Jesus, Peter and John returned to Jerusalem, preaching the gospel in many Samaritan villages.

A new task for Philip

Philip opened the way for Samaria to receive Jesus. Now Peter and John left the new church in Philip's hands and went on to preach in many Samaritan villages. But God has another task for Philip; he calls him to leave this beautiful revival and a new church, to evangelize a single person:

26 Now an angel of the Lord said to Philip, "Go south to the road— the desert road—that goes down from Jerusalem to Gaza."

There is no reason given for this trip. It would be easy to think it was the devil who brought Philip out of a very fertile field of ministry to go into the desert, but it seems that Philip was used to receiving angelic messages. It is a clear command, but very inconvenient. First, he had to walk to Jerusalem (about 43 km, or 27 miles), and then walk in the desert heat to Gaza (no one knows how many kilometers he walked; the whole road would be 79 km, or 49 miles). All of that without knowing why. It sounds crazy.

27 So he started out, and on his way he met an Ethiopian eunuch, an important official in charge of all the treasury of the Kandake (which means "queen of the Ethiopians"). This man had gone to Jerusalem to worship, 28 and on his way home was sitting in his chariot reading the Book of Isaiah the prophet.

Philip did not argue with the angel; he simply obeyed and set out on the journey. That automatic response of obedience opens many opportunities to evangelize and be used by the Lord. God is looking for men and women who are available, and it seems he has a hard time finding them. Maybe none of the apostles in Jerusalem were available. Are you someone God can depend on, whom he can count on to hear his voice and obey it? It should be your goal.

God is sovereign!

The purpose of this detour was to evangelize a high official of the Queen of Ethiopia. A godly man, he had traveled some 4,220 km (2,622 miles) to worship in Jerusalem. And (by chance!) he was reading Isaiah.

When we walk in obedience to the Lord, he prepares the way before us. He will prepare people and send you to them, or bring them to you. Are you willing to walk hours in the desert heat to evangelize a single person? God starts with small things, and when he notices our obedience, he gives us increasingly important opportunities. This was a very important task. Tradition is that this man brought the gospel to Ethiopia and established a church that remains to this day.

29 The Spirit told Philip, "Go to that chariot and stay near it."

Many times, we want a broad vision of God's will: "What ministry do you have for me? Who am I going to marry? What is the purpose of my life?" However, often God guides us step by step, waiting for our obedience to the first step, before directing us to the next one. Do you think God can guide you as clearly as he guided Philip here? Do you have the faith to obey and approach someone you do not know?

30 Then Philip ran up to the chariot and heard the man reading Isaiah the prophet. "Do you understand what you are reading?" Philip asked.

God did not tell Philip what to say, but he gives us common sense. We have to look at what is happening with the person, and for an opening to talk about Jesus. Here it is obvious: He was reading the prophet Isaiah. It is always a good question for someone you see reading the Bible or Christian literature: "Do you understand what you are reading?"

[31] *"How can I," he said, "unless someone explains it to me?" So he invited Philip to come up and sit with him.*

The door is open. When someone invites you to share Christ, take the opportunity! Sit down with them—what a blessing after hours walking in the sun! That is why it is so important to know the Bible, be able to answer questions, and explain what the Word says.

[32] *This is the passage of Scripture the eunuch was reading:*

> *"He was led like a sheep to the slaughter,*
> *and as a lamb before its shearer is silent,*
> *so he did not open his mouth.*
> [33] *In his humiliation he was deprived of justice.*
> *Who can speak of his descendants?*
> *For his life was taken from the earth."*

[34] *The eunuch asked Philip, "Tell me, please, who is the prophet talking about, himself or someone else?"* [35] *Then Philip began with that very passage of Scripture and told him the good news about Jesus.*

Again, we see the Lord's hand leading the eunuch to one of the clearest passages about the Messiah in the Old Testament (Isaiah 53). It is an excellent chapter for evangelizing a Jew, and a very special chapter for the eunuch. Why? I had always thought: "How beautiful. This was a special man. A worshiper of God. A high official of the queen. A very blessed man." God had blessed him, but he was a eunuch. He was not a man, in the way we understand being a man. He was sold or taken from his home as a child, and his testicles were removed. He could never marry or have children. He was despised and rejected among men, a man of sorrows, experienced in brokenness and grief. This eunuch traveled to Jerusalem searching for hope and answers, and now he returned home reading about another man who was despised and rejected. Another man who never had sex with a woman. But who could it be? Now Philip introduces him to Jesus Christ. Of course, this eunuch wants to receive Jesus!

36 As they traveled along the road, they came to some water and the eunuch said, "Look, here is water. What can stand in the way of my being baptized?"

There they are, in the middle of the desert, and God miraculously provides water just in time for the eunuch to accept Christ. And he wants to be baptized!

37 Philip said, "If you believe with all your heart, you may." The eunuch answered, "I believe that Jesus Christ is the Son of God."

Water baptism is important. In Acts, in the early church, people were almost always baptized when they received Christ, the day of Pentecost in Acts 2, and Paul and Silas with the jailer and his family in Acts 16. There is value in classes to ensure someone understands salvation and baptism, but they did not give classes in Acts. At Pentecost, Peter said that the condition is repentance; here Philip says that you have to believe with all your heart, and the eunuch made that confession of faith. There is no biblical foundation for infant baptism; a baby cannot repent or have faith. Have you been baptized in water as a believer?

38 And he gave orders to stop the chariot. Then both Philip and the eunuch went down into the water and Philip baptized him. 39 When they came up out of the water, the Spirit of the Lord suddenly took Philip away, and the eunuch did not see him again, but went on his way rejoicing. 40 Philip, however, appeared at Azotus and traveled about, preaching the gospel in all the towns until he reached Caesarea.

When Philip finished his task, the Spirit took him away. This was a popular verse in prisons: the possibility of being miraculously taken elsewhere! It is always good to provide follow-up (and it is easier today with WhatsApp and social networks), but in this case, the Holy Spirit would have to provide it.

Azotus was one of the main cities of the Philistines, about 35 km (22 miles) from Gaza. The road to Caesarea would be 105 km (65 miles), which gave Philip many opportunities to evangelize. In Acts 21, twenty-five years later, Paul stayed at Philip's house in Caesarea. Philip established the church there and had four unmarried daughters who prophesied.

One man available to God was responsible for the transformation of an entire city and the conversion of an important man who brought the gospel to Ethiopia. God can do the same with you. Do you have the ears to hear his voice? Are you available and willing to obey him? It is an essential part of walking as Jesus walked.

10

Who is Available to Minister to Saul?

Acts 9:9–31

We have seen several examples of God's sovereign work and the impressive way he can use someone available to him, but we are left with questions:

- How could God allow the cruel death of Stephen, one of his very special servants?
- How could he allow Saul to do so much damage to the community of faith?

Is there something in your life that is hard to understand? Despite all your prayers, the person doesn't change and the difficult situation is not resolved.

In this passage, we will see more of how the Lord works and what it means to walk as Jesus walked. This is the second of three conversions which God sovereignly orchestrated. Each one had a significant purpose:

- A man who would take the gospel to Ethiopia (Philip and the eunuch).

- Saul, who became the great apostle Paul, brought the gospel to the Gentiles.
- In the next chapter, Cornelius, whose conversion opened Peter's heart—and the church—to the inclusion of the Gentiles.

God is making sure that the church spreads throughout the world.

Saul tries to destroy the church

¹Meanwhile, Saul was still breathing out murderous threats against the Lord's disciples. He went to the high priest ² and asked him for letters to the synagogues in Damascus, so that if he found any there who belonged to the Way, whether men or women, he might take them as prisoners to Jerusalem.

There are many hardened people in the world, bent on evil and harming the kingdom of God. Saul looks like a lost cause. Full of religious zeal, he is determined to eliminate this heretical sect. Years later, when he recounted his testimony, he said that he was *violently opposed to them* and *obsessed with persecuting them* (Acts 26:11, NLT & NIV). Is there someone in your life who is that hardened against the gospel and seems like a lost cause?

It is not enough that Saul was responsible for a great persecution in Jerusalem; now he wants to "cleanse" all the Jewish communities of the empire of Christians, and he has the support of the high priest and Jewish leaders. It was unusual to arrest women—it was usually the men who suffered for their faith, but Saul was so zealous that he pursued both men and women. It would be difficult to kill them outside Judea, but Saul obtained extradition letters to take them to Jerusalem and kill them there. Nothing and no one was about to stop this man!

This is the first time in the Bible that the name "The Way" is used for Christians (it also appears in Acts 19:9, 23; 22:4; 24:14, 22). It was an appropriate name: Jesus said, *"I am the Way, the Truth and the Life"* (Jn. 14:6); these believers had found the only true way to life.

Sovereign intervention

³ As he neared Damascus on his journey, suddenly a light from heaven flashed around him. ⁴ He fell to the ground and heard a voice say to him, "Saul, Saul, why do you persecute me?"

⁵ "Who are you, Lord?" Saul asked.

"I am Jesus, whom you are persecuting," he replied. ⁶ "Now get up and go into the city, and you will be told what you must do."

God waited until he almost reached his destination, a journey of about 241 kilometers (150 miles). We may not understand the Lord's timing, but he always has his purposes. With someone as hardened as Saul, whom no one can touch with the Word, God is very capable of revealing himself and doing what is necessary to save him. Seeing that light and hearing that voice had to be overwhelming—it was a transformative moment for Paul, who always included it in his testimony.

Jesus' question for Saul was *"why do you persecute me?"* Saul replied, *"Who are you, Lord?"* You may feel confident that you have never persecuted Jesus, but Christ says that to persecute his church is to persecute him.

Years later, in front of King Agrippa, Paul shared more of what happened that day (Acts 26):

⁹ "I too was convinced that I ought to do all that was possible to oppose the name of Jesus of Nazareth. ¹⁰ And that is just what I did in Jerusalem. On the authority of the chief priests I put many *of the Lord's people in prison, and when they were put to death, I cast my vote against them. ¹¹ Many a time I went from one synagogue to another to have them punished, and I tried to force them to blaspheme. I was so obsessed with persecuting them that I even hunted them down in foreign cities.*

¹² "On one of these journeys I was going to Damascus with the authority and commission of the chief priests. ¹³ About noon, King Agrippa, as I was on the road, I saw a light from heaven, brighter than the sun, blazing around me and my companions. ¹⁴ We all fell to the ground, and I heard a voice saying to me in Aramaic 'Saul, Saul, why do you persecute me? It is hard for you to kick against the goads.'

¹⁵ "Then I asked, 'Who are you, Lord?'

" 'I am Jesus, whom you are persecuting,' the Lord replied. ¹⁶ 'Now get up and stand on your feet. I have appeared to you to appoint you as a servant and as a witness of what you have seen and will see of me. ¹⁷ I will rescue you from your own people and from the Gentiles. I am sending you to them ¹⁸ to open their eyes and turn them from darkness to light, and from the power of Satan to God, so that they may receive forgiveness of sins and a place among those who are sanctified by faith in me.'

There are two important things here that do not appear in Chapter 9:

1. Jesus tells him: "*It is hard for you to kick against the goads.*" Other versions say: "*You are hurting yourself by hitting back, like an ox kicking against its owner's stick*" (GNB) or "*It is useless for you to fight against my will*" (NLT). Although he did not expect Jesus to meet him on the road, Paul may have seen Jesus before his crucifixion, and had been fighting God's call for some time. He was troubled and struggling with doubts, because in his quest for

God's righteousness, he felt helpless against the desires of his flesh. Had he been convicted by Stephen's words and appearance the day they stoned him?

Many of us know how hard it is to kick against the goads. Is there any area of your life right now where you are hurting yourself because you are fighting God's will?

2. What was God's purpose in this encounter? Saul's salvation and the blessing of knowing this Christ whom he had persecuted, but even greater, the ministry that Saul would have to the Gentiles. Saul was not seeking God, but God had already called him while he was in his mother's womb. God is sovereign, and there are times when he calls and touches someone. Surely, many Christians were also fervently praying for his salvation (or death!). Saul was not given much choice on that Damascus road. Does that mean we do not have free will? No, but God can be compelling! How have you seen God's sovereign call and work in your life? How does that balance out with how you have acted in your free will? What do you think was God's greater purpose in saving you?

Like Abraham leaving home for the Promised Land, God did not reveal everything to Saul at once. He had to get up, go to the city (humiliated, instead of breathing death), and wait for the next step. He could have rebelled, not gone to Damascus, and returned to Jerusalem, but that would really be kicking against the goads. It is much better to follow what the Lord tells you to do—if you have ever fought with God, you already know how hard it is.

7 The men traveling with Saul stood there speechless; they heard the sound but did not see anyone. 8 Saul got up from the ground, but when he opened his eyes he could see nothing. So they led him by the hand into Damascus. ⁹ For three days he was blind, and did not eat or drink anything.

This highly educated man was like a baby. He didn't know anything. He didn't know if his vision would be restored. Something prompted him not to eat or drink anything, although he did not know how long he would have to fast.

God did what no man could do. He could sovereignly restore his vision and baptize him in the Spirit, with no one else involved, but God prefers to use us. It would be important for Saul to receive the ministry of a Christian brother, and it would be an opportunity for Ananias to grow in his faith.

A man available to minister to the Christian killer

¹⁰ In Damascus there was a disciple named Ananias. The Lord called to him in a vision, "Ananias!"

"Yes, Lord," he answered.

Do you think God still speaks in visions? Why not? The question is whether we are listening. God always looks for available men and women to do his will. There are many things he wants to do in this world, but just as Jesus said: *"The harvest is plentiful, but the workers are few"* (Lk. 10:2). Do you have Ananias' attitude? "Yes, Lord, here am I, send me." He didn't know how difficult this task would be, but when God calls us, he equips us and prepares the way before us.

¹¹ The Lord told him, "Go to the house of Judas on Straight Street and ask for a man from Tarsus named Saul, for he is praying. ¹² In a vision he has seen a man named Ananias come and place his hands on him to restore his sight."

What did Saul do those three days, blind and fasting? He was praying! And God continued to reveal himself in visions. Saul was blind, but now he could see more than ever. Saul was already waiting for an Ananias! It would be hard to refuse this task! Had Ananias ever prayed for someone to regain their sight? We do not know, but God told Ananias exactly what to do and where to go—Straight Street is still one of the main streets in Damascus.

13 "Lord," Ananias answered, "I have heard many reports about this man and all the harm he has done to your holy people in Jerusalem. 14 And he has come here with authority from the chief priests to arrest all who call on your name."

Ananias was not the first to question a call from the Lord. God allows questions; how he responds depends on the person (think about Moses, Zechariah, and Mary, and how he responded to doubts about their call). Probably all the believers in Damascus already knew that Saul wanted to take them as prisoners to Jerusalem, and were praying and fearful. Believers had spread the news about the evil he had done throughout the empire. Poor Ananias was afraid; it seemed like a trap. Maybe it was the devil talking to him?

15 But the Lord said to Ananias, "Go! This man is my chosen instrument to proclaim my name to the Gentiles and their kings and to the people of Israel. 16 I will show him how much he must suffer for my name."

God does not give you an easy out. Perhaps no one else was available to do this important task. We never hear anything more about Ananias, but this humble disciple had the privilege of ministering to one of God's generals. Paul would have a very impressive ministry, but it was also God's purpose that he suffer for the name of Jesus (perhaps because he had persecuted him so much?).

17 Then Ananias went to the house and entered it. Placing his hands on Saul, he said, "Brother Saul, the Lord—Jesus, who appeared to you on the road as you were coming here—has sent me so that you may see again and be filled with the Holy Spirit." 18 Immediately, something like scales fell from Saul's eyes, and he could see again. He got up and was baptized, 19 and after taking some food, he regained his strength.

We do not know the details of what happened. Did Ananias go in fear, or with authority and confidence? The important thing is that he obeyed. Obedience is evidence of our faith—emotions do not matter that much. God honored that obedience and did the work. Despite his fears, he called Saul "brother," probably the first time Saul heard that term of affection applied to himself. God did not mention the Holy Spirit when he called Ananias (v. 12), but the Lord baptized Paul in the Spirit, probably when Ananias laid hands on him in his water baptism. Perhaps Saul regained his sight when Ananias proclaimed that word. He was weak, but he ate and was strengthened. We can only imagine Ananias' amazement and joy, and that first fellowship, now as brothers in Christ. It does not say what happened to the men who accompanied Saul from Jerusalem; possibly they also received Christ, or maybe returned fearfully to Jerusalem to share the news with the priests.

Saul preaches in the synagogues of Damascus

Saul spent several days with the disciples in Damascus. 20 At once he began to preach in the synagogues that Jesus is the Son of God. 21 All those who heard him were astonished and asked, "Isn't he the man who raised havoc in Jerusalem among those who call on this name? And hasn't he come here to take them as prisoners to the chief priests?" 22 Yet Saul grew more and more powerful and baffled the Jews living in Damascus by proving that Jesus is the Messiah.

Usually, we give a new convert time to get established, demonstrate a transformed life, and study the word. Sadly, there are stories of famous people who receive the Lord and go out preaching and ministering right away. They are targets for the devil, lack a firm foundation in the Lord, and often end up in trouble. Paul was a special case; as a Pharisee, he already had training and knowledge of the Word, and now he was filled with the Holy Spirit. I have seen men saved in prison who preach the Word with anointing within a few days. God can raise someone up when he wants to.

Although his call was to the Gentiles, logically—as he always did on his missionary trips—he first went to the synagogues, proclaiming Jesus Christ as their Messiah. They were astonished and baffled by his preaching.

23 After many days had gone by, there was a conspiracy among the Jews to kill him, 24 but Saul learned of their plan. Day and night they kept close watch on the city gates in order to kill him. 25 But his followers took him by night and lowered him in a basket through an opening in the wall.

When someone challenges our beliefs and threatens our position, we want to get rid of them. This was the first of many near-death experiences for Saul; he was already learning how much he had to suffer for the name of Christ.

We know from Galatians 1:17–18 that the *"many days"* were three and a half years spent in "Arabia," probably a time of study and preparation in the desert near Damascus. Interestingly, he says that *"his followers* (or *disciples*)" helped him escape. It seems that in those *"many days,"* he already established himself as a skilled teacher of the Scriptures.

²⁶ *When he came to Jerusalem, he tried to join the disciples, but they were all afraid of him, not believing that he really was a disciple.*

Those who were praying should have been full of faith, rejoicing in this man's transformation, but they were afraid of him! It is hard when someone wants to join the church, but because of their previous life, Christians are afraid to receive them! Someone had to take him to the "apostles" to receive their support, and Barnabas, that special man who already appeared at the end of chapter 4, befriended him. Do you have that Barnabas heart to help someone?

²⁷ *But Barnabas took him and brought him to the apostles. He told them how Saul on his journey had seen the Lord and that the Lord had spoken to him, and how in Damascus he had preached fearlessly in the name of Jesus. ²⁸ So Saul stayed with them and moved about freely in Jerusalem, speaking boldly in the name of the Lord. ²⁹ He talked and debated with the Hellenistic Jews, but they tried to kill him. ³⁰ When the believers learned of this, they took him down to Caesarea and sent him off to Tarsus.*

Thank God for his boldness and obedience to preach. It must have shocked the priests and religious leaders who sent him to arrest the disciples in Damascus. For the second time, the Jews wanted to kill him, but he escaped to his hometown of Tarsus.

Summary: The state of the Church

³¹ *Then the church throughout Judea, Galilee and Samaria enjoyed a time of peace and was strengthened. Living in the fear of the Lord and encouraged by the Holy Spirit, it increased in numbers.*

Characteristic of what we have already seen in Acts, this section ends with another update on the status of the church. The portion began in chapter 6 and includes the first persecution, the first time the gospel reaches the Gentiles (the Samaritans), and the conversion of Saul, the apostle to the Gentiles. With his conversion, the persecution ends, and again there is peace.

Now the Jerusalem church (apart from believers elsewhere, like Ananias in Damascus) was consolidating, not only in Judea, but also in Galilee and Samaria. They had peace, but it seems that they also had a new respect for God, living in the fear of the Lord. Their number continued to grow, due to the work of the Holy Spirit, who strengthened and empowered them to testify about Jesus.

Your Damascus road

Have you met Jesus as Saul did on the Damascus road? Or are you still hurting yourself, kicking against the goads? Saul was a very educated and religious man. He was on his way to do what he believed to be God's will, but he was wrong. I have met pastors who realize they have served God their own way, but have never had a genuine conversion. Not every conversion is as dramatic as Saul's, but it is important to have that encounter with Jesus and be born again.

Saul's conversion is a powerful affirmation of the reality of the living Christ. Saul was a skeptic. He needed something powerful to convince him that Christ was his messiah. There is no doubt that Saul was a real man, a Pharisee, who lived in the first century, planted many churches, and wrote letters that are part of our Bibles. It is normal to have doubts at times, but this story (and the entire book of Acts) is a solid confirmation of the truth of what we believe.

11

Peter's First Missionary Journey

Acts 9:32–10:23

If someone is really seeking God and wants to know the truth, the Lord can go to extraordinary lengths to reveal himself and lead that person to salvation. There are many testimonies today of Christ appearing to someone in dreams, especially among Muslims. We have already seen two examples of God's sovereign move in Acts:

- He sent Philip on a long desert journey to introduce the eunuch to Jesus, and even supplied the water to baptize him!
- With Saul, it was a revelation of the living Christ and a complete interruption of his life. Ananias was the disciple God used to minister to Saul.

God was laying the groundwork for the inclusion of the Gentiles in the church and the resulting massive growth. He already had his apostle/missionary (Saul/Paul), but he still had to change Peter's mind. He was the leader of the apostles, but he was a hard one to convince, and would require a revelation almost as dramatic as Saul's, a vision that would allow him to travel to a Gentile's home. However, first, God had to get him in the vicinity, so Peter embarked on his first real missionary journey, where he would have the opportunity to heal a paralytic and raise a dead woman.

Peter heals a paralytic in Lydda

Jesus was always on the move—he traveled throughout Judea and Galilee and even the neighboring regions. Apostolic ministry also involves travel. Here, unlike what we have usually seen in Acts, Peter traveled alone. A simple visit to the church in Lydda resulted in a healing that sparked explosive growth:

[32] As Peter traveled about the country, he went to visit the Lord's people who lived in Lydda. [33] There he found a man named Aeneas, who was paralyzed and had been bedridden for eight years. [34] "Aeneas," Peter said to him, "Jesus Christ heals you. Get up and roll up your mat." Immediately Aeneas got up. [35] All those who lived in Lydda and Sharon saw him and turned to the Lord.

If we are looking for a formula to minister healing, there is none. With the paralytic in Acts 3, Peter said, "In the name of Jesus." Here, he says, *"Jesus Christ heals you."* It really is the same; in both cases, it is clear that it is Jesus who heals. Peter says *"get up"* to both of them, but here he does not have to extend his hand. He simply tells him to get up, and curiously, adds that he should roll up his mat, perhaps to confirm that he will no longer need it. Here again, the healing is instantaneous, although that is not always the case.

Aeneas left the house, telling everyone that Jesus healed him. In these small towns, the news spreads quickly; *"everyone"* who lived in those villages saw him and believed in Jesus. Again, we see how a miracle draws people's attention; of course, they want to meet this miracle worker. An impressive expansion of the church started as a simple visit to the saints. The NIV says *"the Lord's people,"* but the Greek says "saints." Biblically, all believers are saints. The miracle confirmed the word that those saints were already sharing.

Dorcas raised from the dead

36 In Joppa there was a disciple named Tabitha (in Greek her name is Dorcas); she was always doing good and helping the poor. 37 About that time she became sick and died, and her body was washed and placed in an upstairs room. 38 Lydda was near Joppa; so when the disciples heard that Peter was in Lydda, they sent two men to him and urged him, "Please come at once!"

While Peter stayed in Lydda, the news of the miracle reached Joppa, a neighboring village, about 18 km (11 miles) away. Apparently, Peter had not visited Joppa, although there was already a church there. One of the older sisters in the church, a widow, Dorcas was known for her good works and helping the poor. Although she was clearly dead, given Peter's reputation, they believed she could still be resurrected. It reminds us of Jesus receiving the news about Lazarus, and waiting to go (Jn. 11), but Peter went *"at once."*

39 Peter went with them, and when he arrived he was taken upstairs to the room. All the widows stood around him, crying and showing him the robes and other clothing that Dorcas had made while she was still with them.

40 Peter sent them all out of the room; then he got down on his knees and prayed. Turning toward the dead woman, he said, "Tabitha, get up." She opened her eyes, and seeing Peter she sat up. 41 He took her by the hand and helped her to her feet. Then he called for the believers, especially the widows, and presented her to them alive.

This is the first record of an apostle raising someone from the dead. First, Peter had everyone leave the room, as Jesus did with the resurrection of Jairus' daughter (Mk. 5:40). Peter wanted to prepare and focus in prayer; probably in that time of communion with his Master, he received confirmation that Jesus wanted to resurrect her. Unlike the previous two healings, Peter does not mention the name of Jesus; possibly, in those cases, he said it for the benefit of the others. Peter simply commands her: *Get up.* As he did with the cripple in chapter 3, he took her hand and helped her up. Imagine the thrill when he presented her alive to the believers and widows!

⁴² This became known all over Joppa, and many people believed in the Lord. ⁴³ Peter stayed in Joppa for some time with a tanner named Simon.

Thus, his ministry at Lydda ended; now he has many new believers to disciple at Joppa, the result of Dorcas' testimony.

An angel visits a Roman centurion

¹⁰:¹At Caesarea there was a man named Cornelius, a centurion in what was known as the Italian Regiment. ² He and all his family were devout and God-fearing; he gave generously to those in need and prayed to God regularly.

Jesus recognized a centurion's great faith that resulted in the healing of his servant (Matt. 8:5–13), but this is the first Roman mentioned in Acts. He is a man of prayer, God-fearing, and a family man. He gave generously to the Jews, and his entire family was devout. God wanted to bless him, but how? When God wants to do something, he looks for someone available and then goes about putting everything in place.

³ One day at about three in the afternoon he had a vision. He distinctly saw an angel of God, who came to him and said, "Cornelius!"

We already know that three in the afternoon is the hour of prayer for the Jews. He was probably praying, in an attitude to receive from the Lord. I am intrigued when someone says, "I want to hear from God," but always has the television, internet, or headphones of his cell phone filling his eyes, ears, and mind. In order to receive a vision, it is important to be in an appropriate place—or, like Saul, be thrown to the ground by the impact of the blazing light of God's presence.

God knows your name! He calls you by name and knows you completely.

⁴ Cornelius stared at him in fear. "What is it, Lord?" he asked.

Of course, he was afraid. In the Bible, it is normal to be afraid when the Lord or his angel appears. The stories today of people fearlessly conversing with angels do not strike me as very authentic. Despite his fear, he stared at him. Knowing that he was sent from the Lord, his first instinct was to make himself available: "What do you want, Lord?" He did not ask for anything from the angel; he just wanted to do God's will.

The angel answered, "Your prayers and gifts to the poor have come up as a memorial offering before God. ⁵ Now send men to Joppa to bring back a man named Simon who is called Peter. ⁶ He is staying with Simon the tanner, whose house is by the sea."

First, the angel alleviated his fear. God had received his prayers and his actions to help those in need as an offering and was pleased with Cornelius. We usually think of offerings as money, but your prayers and good works can be an offering to God. It is clear that God had something positive for Cornelius, but he did not tell him what it was. He only gave exact instructions on what to do, and there was urgency: he had to send men immediately.

God knows your name, and he knows where you live and where you are right now.

The angel could preach Jesus to him, but God almost always uses us to evangelize, and Peter's lesson was as important as Cornelius's conversion.

⁷ When the angel who spoke to him had gone, Cornelius called two of his servants and a devout soldier who was one of his attendants. ⁸ He told them everything that had happened and sent them to Joppa.

Cornelius was also obedient. Without asking anything else—unlike Ananias and so many others in the Bible who received a word from God—he sent three trustworthy men to Joppa, about 63 km (39 miles) directly south, along the Mediterranean Sea (Joppa is a suburb of Tel Aviv today).

Cornelius had done his part. His servants were already on their way to Joppa. Now God needs Peter's cooperation. He trusts Peter, just as he trusted Philip and Ananias for their ministry to the eunuch and to Saul.

Peter, hungry, prays and falls into a trance

⁹ About noon the following day as they were on their journey and approaching the city, Peter went up on the roof to pray.

Although it was not the time for prayer, from the roof he could see the sea and communicate with his Lord. It was when Peter set aside time to pray that God could speak to him.

¹⁰ He became hungry and wanted something to eat, and while the meal was being prepared, he fell into a trance.

Peter was only thinking about lunch, but he had to wait while the food was being prepared, so he decided to pray. There, in the Lord's presence, he fell into a trance and received a very impressive vision. Sometimes the message has a stronger impact when we see it, almost like a movie.

¹¹ He saw heaven opened and something like a large sheet being let down to earth by its four corners. ¹² It contained all kinds of four-footed animals, as well as reptiles and birds. ¹³ Then a voice told him, "Get up, Peter. Kill and eat."

¹⁴ "Surely not, Lord!" Peter replied. "I have never eaten anything impure or unclean."

Could it be a test? He recognized the voice; Peter called him "*Lord*." Peter knew Jesus intimately. Why didn't the Lord just speak to him? Why the mystery? We may not understand it, but many times God speaks to us like this. The voice told him to break a law that he had kept all his life.

¹⁵ The voice spoke to him a second time, "Do not call anything impure that God has made clean."

¹⁶ This happened three times, and immediately the sheet was taken back to heaven.

God did not rebuke him or explain the message, although it was clear: Animals that could not be eaten under the Law, impure animals, had been purified, and Peter could eat them. This would be a radical change in the interpretation of the Law and how it is applied to the Christian.

¹⁷ While Peter was wondering about the meaning of the vision, the men sent by Cornelius found out where Simon's house was and stopped at the gate. ¹⁸ They called out, asking if Simon who was known as Peter was staying there.

Have you had that happen, at what seems the wrong time? You may be meditating on the Word or in prayer, and your wife or children call you, someone comes to the door, or you receive a phone call. Why didn't God allow him to reflect on the vision and understand it?

19 While Peter was still thinking about the vision, the Spirit said to him, "Simon, three men are looking for you. 20 So get up and go downstairs. Do not hesitate to go with them, for I have sent them."

To make it more complicated, the Spirit now told him that he should accompany the three men who had just arrived at the house. He did not tell him why; only that he had to obey in a hurry. God was organizing everything, and Peter had a key part. Already confused by the vision, now he had to go with three men, probably Romans, whom he did not know. How exciting to hear the voice of the Spirit like this and participate in the Lord's work! You can too!

21 Peter went down and said to the men, "I'm the one you're looking for. Why have you come?"

Peter did not argue with the Lord, but accepted that it was from God. He had the attitude that we should always have when God calls us to do something: Here am I, Lord. Send me.

22 The men replied, "We have come from Cornelius the centurion. He is a righteous and God-fearing man, who is respected by all the Jewish people. A holy angel told him to ask you to come to his house so that he could hear what you have to say." 23 Then Peter invited the men into the house to be his guests.

It would be hard to refuse that invitation; it was an open door for ministry. There was only one caveat for Peter: A Jew should not have Gentiles in his house or eat with them.

What would you do? Has God provided similar opportunities for you? Are you available to God and obedient to his voice? Is there a time in your day when God has your attention and can speak to you?

12

Peter in Cornelius' House

Acts 10:23–48

Peter did not have much choice after God so clearly spoke to him. God wants to overcome our prejudices so we can welcome all kinds of people into our lives. The Pharisees condemned Jesus for the "sinners" he hung out with, but Jesus seemed to feel much more comfortable with them than with "religious" people who were quick to judge others.

23 Then Peter invited the men into the house to be his guests. The next day Peter started out with them, and some of the believers from Joppa went along. 24 The following day he arrived in Caesarea. Cornelius was expecting them and had called together his relatives and close friends.

It did not seem like that long a journey, but it had already been four days since Cornelius received the vision. Peter allowed these Gentiles to spend the night in the house at Joppa, and now they were going to Caesarea together. I would love to know what they were talking about on the way! Jesus must have been smiling at Peter's new experience!

Cornelius had great faith that Peter would come, and must have had some idea of when it would be. The vision had impressed him deeply, and he gathered his relatives and close friends at his house. How tragic if Peter ignored the voice of the Spirit and refused to go to a Gentile's home! How tragic when God prepares someone's heart who is sincerely seeking the Lord, and, because of our disobedience, no one shares the gospel with them!

Peter arrives at Cornelius' house

25 As Peter entered the house, Cornelius met him and fell at his feet in reverence. 26 But Peter made him get up. "Stand up," he said, "I am only a man myself."

Peter was about to abandon the prejudice against the Gentiles that was instilled in him as a Jewish child. He was used to people's praise; they wanted his shadow to fall on them to receive a healing. It could be tempting to welcome the centurion's recognition, but Peter had learned from the Master and knew that we are all equal before God. You should never pay homage to another man. Be careful of accepting the worship of people you minister to. They may not prostrate themselves before you, but there are pastors, apostles, and other ministers who allow or even encourage this elevation above the common people of the church.

27 While talking with him, Peter went inside and found a large gathering of people. 28 He said to them: "You are well aware that it is against our law for a Jew to associate with or visit a Gentile. But God has shown me that I should not call anyone impure or unclean. 29 So when I was sent for, I came without raising any objection. May I ask why you sent for me?"

It seems strange that Peter could not discern what to do through the Spirit; it would seem obvious that he should share God's love and the good news of salvation. Given the respect and honor that

Cornelius showed him, Peter's response seemed abrupt, as if he were saying: "This is the first time I have ever entered a Gentile's house. I am only here because of a revelation from God, but I really do not understand why you had me make this long trip."

30 Cornelius answered: "Three days ago I was in my house praying at this hour, at three in the afternoon. Suddenly a man in shining clothes stood before me 31 and said, 'Cornelius, God has heard your prayer and remembered your gifts to the poor. 32 Send to Joppa for Simon who is called Peter. He is a guest in the home of Simon the tanner, who lives by the sea.' 33 So I sent for you immediately, and it was good of you to come. Now we are all here in the presence of God to listen to everything the Lord has commanded you to tell us."

This man's tender, open heart was evident. He was grateful that Peter came. He knew (perhaps better than Peter!) that they were in God's presence, and was confident that God had given Peter an important message to share with them.

Peter preaches

34 Then Peter began to speak: "I now realize how true it is that God does not show favoritism 35 but accepts from every nation the one who fears him and does what is right. 36 You know the message God sent to the people of Israel, announcing the good news of peace through Jesus Christ, who is Lord of all. 37 You know what has happened throughout the province of Judea, beginning in Galilee after the baptism that John preached— 38 how God anointed Jesus of Nazareth with the Holy Spirit and power, and how he went around doing good and healing all who were under the power of the devil, because God was with him.

39 "We are witnesses of everything he did in the country of the Jews and in Jerusalem. They killed him by hanging him on a cross, 40 but God raised him from the dead on the third day and caused him to be seen. [41] He was not seen by all the people, but by witnesses whom God had already chosen—by us who ate and drank with him after he rose from the dead. [42] He commanded us to preach to the people and to testify that he is the one whom God appointed as judge of the living and the dead. [43] All the prophets testify about him that everyone who believes in him receives forgiveness of sins through his name."

Like Peter's other sermons, this is short. It takes about two minutes to preach—although some scholars say it is only a summary of his message. It does not take much time to communicate the Gospel. Peter packed a lot into that brief time. Surely he had not prepared it beforehand, but God gave him the words:

- Introduction: What God revealed to Peter
  - God does not have favorites
  - No matter their nationality, God welcomes:
    - Those who fear him
    - Those who seek righteousness
  - Cornelius is one of those people

- What God started with the people of Israel: The good news of peace through Jesus Christ
  - The Gospel
    - Jesus' ministry started with John's baptism
    - It originated in Galilee, in Nazareth
    - It spread throughout Judea
    - The good news has already reached Caesarea
  - Who Jesus is
    - Anointed by God with the Holy Spirit and power

- Worker of good deeds
- Healer of all whom the devil oppressed
- God was with Him
- Killed by the Jews, who hung him on a tree
- Raised by God on the third day
- The judge of the living and the dead

- The apostles' role
  - Witnesses to everything he did; there is no doubt that Jesus physically resurrected
  - Previously chosen by God
  - Ate and drank with him after his resurrection
  - Commanded by Jesus to preach to the people
  - Must bear witness that God has appointed Jesus as judge

- Not only the apostles, but all the prophets bear witness to this salvation
  - It is for all who believe in him
  - It is through his name
  - They will receive forgiveness of sins

The Spirit falls on the Gentiles

⁴⁴ While Peter was still speaking these words, the Holy Spirit came on all who heard the message.

Maybe Peter was about to give an invitation, but it was not necessary. Their hearts were so open, and they received the word with such faith, that the Spirit sovereignly fell on everyone.

⁴⁵ The circumcised believers who had come with Peter were astonished that the gift of the Holy Spirit had been poured out even on Gentiles.

God gave Peter a vision that Gentiles were to be part of the Kingdom, but he was with other Jews from Joppa who were uncomfortable in a Gentile house. Like most Jews, they could not believe that God would bless someone who was uncircumcised. They did not expect that Cornelius and the others could get saved, let alone receive the gift of the Holy Spirit, but God gave the confirmation:

46 For they heard them speaking in tongues and praising God.

Speaking in tongues would only be possible for someone baptized in the Spirit, which Peter and his companions had already received. The joy and praise in that house were like another Pentecost.

Then Peter said, 47 "Surely no one can stand in the way of their being baptized with water. They have received the Holy Spirit just as we have." 48 So he ordered that they be baptized in the name of Jesus Christ. Then they asked Peter to stay with them for a few days.

Again, we see the importance of water baptism. If they already had the baptism in the Spirit, Peter's first instinct was to baptize them in water also. There is no single model for receiving these baptisms. Here, as at Pentecost, baptism in the Spirit was a sovereign gift from God, probably necessary to convince Peter and his companions that they were truly saved.

The wonderful thing in this story is the love of God for someone who sincerely seeks him, and the extraordinary measures the Lord can use to bring salvation to that person. Peter is now their "spiritual father," and of course, they want him to stay with them for a few days. When we walk as Jesus walked, we do not have to prepare an agenda. God sends us wherever he wants, and people receive us and host us. Just like the lame man who held onto Peter and John, these people cannot thank Peter enough. And it has been an unforgettable lesson for Peter: For the first time, he had a Roman centurion as a brother.

Are you available to God? Are you open to challenging common concepts among Christians that are not necessarily biblical?

13

The Church Expands

Acts 11

Those were exciting days for Peter in Caesarea, full of new experiences. Peter stayed in a Gentile's house for the first time, and probably ate food that was not kosher. Cornelius immediately began to share his new faith with his troops, and others accepted Jesus. However, it was one thing to be in the midst of a supernatural move of God and see those people get baptized in the Spirit, and it was another to receive the news from afar.

Critics

¹The apostles and the believers throughout Judea heard that the Gentiles also had received the word of God. ² So when Peter went up to Jerusalem, the circumcised believers criticized him ³ and said, "You went into the house of uncircumcised men and ate with them."

Nothing has changed in two thousand years; there is always someone ready to criticize, and you can imagine the rumors:

- "What happened to Peter? He no longer keeps the law."
- "He was in a Gentile house and someone said they ate shrimp!"

- "We lost him. The devil deceived him. I would not be surprised if he left his wife and moved to Caesarea to live the good life."

When Peter returned home to Jerusalem, he had a lot to explain. If they did not accept it, there could be a division in the church. That has happened too many times throughout history.

Peter defends himself

Thank God, Peter had a chance to defend himself. In the worst cases, a church could simply remove a pastor who "has fallen into sin."

⁴ Starting from the beginning, Peter told them the whole story:

Fortunately, they listened to Peter as he explained what happened. He did not raise his voice or denounce the prejudice of the circumcision group or their ignorance; he patiently shared the whole story with them:

⁵ "I was in the city of Joppa praying, and in a trance I saw a vision. I saw something like a large sheet being let down from heaven by its four corners, and it came down to where I was. ⁶ I looked into it and saw four-footed animals of the earth, wild beasts, reptiles and birds. ⁷ Then I heard a voice telling me, 'Get up, Peter. Kill and eat.'

⁸ "I replied, 'Surely not, Lord! Nothing impure or unclean has ever entered my mouth.'

⁹ "The voice spoke from heaven a second time, 'Do not call anything impure that God has made clean.' ¹⁰ This happened three times, and then it was all pulled up to heaven again.

¹¹ "Right then three men who had been sent to me from Caesarea stopped at the house where I was staying. ¹² The Spirit told me to have no hesitation about going with them. These six brothers also went with me, and we entered the man's house. *¹³ He told us how he had seen an angel appear in his house and say, 'Send to Joppa for Simon who is called Peter. ¹⁴ He will bring you a message through which you and all your household will be saved.'*

That last part was not included in the previous chapter; it was a promise of salvation for his whole family, through the word Peter would bring. That happened with the jailer's family in Philippi as well, and it is the Lord's desire: When the head of the house receives Christ, the whole family follows them and is saved.

¹⁵ "As I began to speak, the Holy Spirit came on them as he had come on us at the beginning. ¹⁶ Then I remembered what the Lord had said: 'John baptized with water, but you will be baptized with the Holy Spirit.' ¹⁷ So if God gave them the same gift he gave us who believed in the Lord Jesus Christ, who was I to think that I could stand in God's way?"

Peter does not present a biblical case for the inclusion of the Gentiles or resolve the question of what foods are allowed for believers. For him, receiving the baptism of the Holy Spirit confirmed the validity of what God did.

¹⁸ When they heard this, they had no further objections and praised God, saying, "So then, even to Gentiles God has granted repentance that leads to life."

Of course, the Spirit was working in those believers' hearts, as they dropped their criticism and praised God for what he had done. It was a giant step: the church would be a religion open to everyone, not only a sect within Judaism.

The status of the church

This is the closing of a portion that relates a major advance: the inclusion of Gentiles in the church. There are also impressive works of the Holy Spirit:

- The problem of Greek-speaking widows and its resolution with the selection of deacons.
- Stephen's martyrdom.
- Philip in Samaria and evangelizing the Ethiopian eunuch.
- Saul's conversion.
- Peter's experience with Cornelius.

Now, as usual when he concludes one portion, Luke gives us an update on the church's status:

[19] Now those who had been scattered by the persecution that broke out when Stephen was killed traveled as far as Phoenicia, Cyprus and Antioch, spreading the word only among Jews. [20] Some of them, however, men from Cyprus and Cyrene, went to Antioch and began to speak to Greeks also, telling them the good news about the Lord Jesus. [21] The Lord's hand was with them, and a great number of people believed and turned to the Lord.

Other cities also received the gospel, and a large number believed, but these brothers were not ready to evangelize the Gentiles; they announced the message only to the Jews. It was in Antioch that a door was opened to include Greek-speakers. Antioch was a beautiful city of about half a million, including Chinese, Indians, and Persians. It was the capital of the Roman province of Syria, and a very cosmopolitan city. Believers from Cyprus and Cyrene brought the gospel to the Greek-speaking Jews and Greeks in Antioch, while continuing to evangelize the Aramaic-speakers. Although Jerusalem was the mother church, it

was already losing some of its influence, along with its ties to the
temple and the Jewish religion.

*²² News of this reached the church in Jerusalem, and they sent
Barnabas to Antioch. ²³ When he arrived and saw what the grace
of God had done, he was glad and encouraged them all to remain
true to the Lord with all their hearts. ²⁴ He was a good man, full of
the Holy Spirit and faith, and a great number of people were
brought to the Lord.*

Barnabas was also from Cyprus, although he lived in Jerusalem.
Just as Peter and John were sent to confirm that everything was
correctly done in Samaria, Barnabas was a logical choice to go to
Antioch and oversee what was happening. He was already
functioning as an apostle. We saw his great heart in the donation
of his land and his support of Saul. Here Luke affirms that, saying
that he was a good man, full of the Holy Spirit and faith. He saw
much evidence of God's grace in Antioch, encouraged the
brothers, and stayed there for a while, evangelizing, and
experiencing a great harvest.

*²⁵ Then Barnabas went to Tarsus to look for Saul, ²⁶ and when he
found him, he brought him to Antioch. So for a whole year
Barnabas and Saul met with the church and taught great
numbers of people. The disciples were called Christians first at
Antioch.*

The usual pattern is to work in pairs, and Barnabas was led to
invite Saul to work with him in Antioch; it is an excellent example
of looking for a younger brother in the faith and taking him to
work with you. It was a true apostolic work, teaching "many
people" for a year. From that ministry, the name "Christian" was
first given to the believers, because Christ was the center of their
faith. Some believe that Luke was among the converts in Antioch,
and his remarkable friendship with Paul started there.

27 During this time, some prophets came down from Jerusalem to Antioch. 28 One of them, named Agabus, stood up and through the Spirit predicted that a severe famine would spread over the entire Roman world. (This happened during the reign of Claudius.) 29 The disciples, as each one was able, decided to provide help for the brothers and sisters living in Judea. 30 This they did, sending their gift to the elders by Barnabas and Saul.

Another part of the exchange between the churches was the ministry of prophets. We do not have the names of most of them and do not know much about their ministry, but they also visited churches in various parts of the world. When Agabus prophesied a great famine, the disciples decided to help the brothers in Judea, a poorer province. It was the first of many offerings that Saul collected to help other churches, this time with Barnabas. It was Saul's second visit to Jerusalem, perhaps the one he describes in Galatians 2:1–10. They were not forced to give; the decision was up to each individual, and it was according to their means.

In these chapters, we have seen a significant expansion of the church's ministry and continued growth. Now there were deacons, apostles, and prophets who visited the disciples, who were further and further from Jerusalem. However, as always, there was opposition from the enemy.

14

One Apostle Dead, Another Saved

Acts 12:1–24

THere had been a radical turn in "The Way." Far from the "Promised Land" or the "Holy Land," believers were called "Christians" for the first time in Antioch. Although Jerusalem remained the mother church, an unstoppable expansion had begun among the Gentiles. In another thirty years, in AD 70, the temple and Jerusalem will be destroyed. The second half of Acts recounts Paul's ministry all the way to the capital of the empire; in a few years, that church would be the most important in the world. Rome, the seat of the Catholic Church (the largest on earth), has not lost that status. No other city today has that much influence over Christians.

In the meantime, however, important things were happening in Jerusalem. Since Pentecost, the Jewish religious leaders had sporadically persecuted the church, but there were few problems with the ruling Romans. When that persecution came, some ten years after Jesus' crucifixion, it had nothing to do with religion, but with maintaining the king's power. More often than not, persecutions by the government have little to do with religion.

The first martyr of the twelve apostles

¹It was about this time that King Herod arrested some who belonged to the church, intending to persecute them. ² He had James, the brother of John, put to death with the sword.

Herod Agrippa was Herod the Great's grandson; his uncle, Herod Antipas, had met Jesus. The support of the religious establishment (the Sadducees and the priests) was critical to him, so he arrested some believers and killed James. It appears to have caught the church off guard; when they woke up, James was already dead. Oddly, for something so important, Luke says almost nothing about it.

James was one of the three closest disciples of Jesus Christ (along with his brother John and Peter), yet we have heard nothing about him, other than to name him among those in the upper room (Acts 1:13). Another James, Jesus' half-brother, was the head of the Jerusalem church. James was the first of the twelve apostles to die (aside from Judas Iscariot), and although Luke does not say anything more, it must have been a cruel blow to John, Peter, and the whole church.

³ When [Herod] saw that this met with approval among the Jews, he proceeded to seize Peter also. This happened during the Festival of Unleavened Bread.

Peter was able to escape James' fate because he was arrested during Passover (Jesus was arrested just before Passover).

⁴ After arresting him, he put him in prison, handing him over to be guarded by four squads of four soldiers each. Herod intended to bring him out for public trial after the Passover.

This was maximum custody; Herod did not want any chance of escape, and God allowed it to glorify himself and demonstrate that there is nothing difficult for him.

The power of prayer

⁵ So Peter was kept in prison, but the church was earnestly praying to God for him.

We have seen the importance of the "but," and this "but" is very important. The king can do whatever he wants, but he is no match for God's power. Had the church gotten a little lax in its prayer? When they arrested James and the others, were they not praying fervently? Could James' death have awakened the church to the importance of prayer? Christians can get comfortable and neglect prayer. We might say that God still had plans and tasks for Peter and would not allow Herod to kill him, but God honors and responds to the prayers of his people, and Luke makes a point of saying they prayed *earnestly* (AMP: *fervently*). God had already rescued Peter (and John) once (Acts 5:19)–the church had faith that he could do it again.

What do you need to get you praying constantly and fervently? Unfortunately, it is often a serious illness, marital problems, or a wayward child. We wait for the crisis to pray.

⁶ The night before Herod was to bring him to trial, Peter was sleeping between two soldiers, bound with two chains, and sentries stood guard at the entrance.

Peter spent several days in prison. God could have freed him the first night, but he wanted to build the faith of Peter and the believers, give the church a chance to pray, and possibly give Peter a chance to witness to the soldiers. It was not until Herod was about to bring him to trial that God acted.

Nothing is said about Peter's attitude or faith during those days. Surely he knew that he could experience the same end as James or Jesus. Luke emphasizes the maximum security provided for this dangerous man. We only know that he was asleep that night—he was not praying, but he was not so anxious that he could not sleep. There are times when even the most anointed person cannot pray. Thank God we are part of a body, and others can pray when you cannot. Do not hesitate to share your needs with others so they can pray, and hold up others in chains who can benefit from your prayers.

Peter's miraculous deliverance

⁷ Suddenly an angel of the Lord appeared and a light shone in the cell. He struck Peter on the side and woke him up. "Quick, get up!" he said, and the chains fell off Peter's wrists. ⁸ Then the angel said to him, "Put on your clothes and sandals." And Peter did so. "Wrap your cloak around you and follow me," the angel told him.

The angel appeared and the light shone, but the soldiers were clueless; God hid it from them—a pity, because they paid for their innocent lapse with their lives. It was God's sovereign intervention. Peter was still half asleep and did not understand what was happening, but he obeyed the angel.

⁹ Peter followed him out of the prison, but he had no idea that what the angel was doing was really happening; he thought he was seeing a vision. ¹⁰ They passed the first and second guards and came to the iron gate leading to the city. It opened for them by itself, and they went through it. When they had walked the length of one street, suddenly the angel left him.

Peter was groggy; was this a dream, or reality? God's power is amazing! He blinded the guards and opened the gate.

Peter looks for the believers

¹¹ Then Peter came to himself and said, "Now I know without a doubt that the Lord has sent his angel and rescued me from Herod's clutches and from everything the Jewish people were hoping would happen."

Now he was awake and realized he was free. So where did he go?

12 When this had dawned on him, he went to the house of Mary the mother of John, also called Mark, where many people had gathered and were praying.

The early church often met in homes (there were no church buildings). It was very late, but the house was full of people praying. John Mark was a companion of Peter's (he called him his "son," 1 Peter 5:13). Possibly he was in the garden the night of Jesus' arrest and fled naked (Mrk. 14:51). He was a cousin of Barnabas, traveled with Paul, and wrote the Gospel of Mark (based on Peter's input). This was an important family in the Jerusalem church. Unfortunately, as is often true in today's church, the father is not mentioned; we do not know if he was not around, or just not interested in church.

At the very moment that God released Peter, they were praying.

13 Peter knocked at the outer entrance, and a servant named Rhoda came to answer the door. 14 When she recognized Peter's voice, she was so overjoyed she ran back without opening it and exclaimed, "Peter is at the door!"

Peter expected the police at any moment and was eager to get out of the street, but Rhoda did not open the door, even though she recognized him.

15 "You're out of your mind," they told her. When she kept insisting that it was so, they said, "It must be his angel."

Why is it that we pray without expecting an answer to our prayers? They spent several days constantly praying fervently, and when the answer to their request appeared at the door, they said the person bringing the news was crazy!

16 But Peter kept on knocking, and when they opened the door and saw him, they were astonished. 17 Peter motioned with his hand for them to be quiet and described how the Lord had brought him out of prison. "Tell James and the other brothers and sisters about this," he said, and then he left for another place.

Just like the disciples when Jesus appeared to them after his resurrection, they were stunned. There is an interesting detail here: Peter wanted them to tell James (obviously not John's brother, but Jesus' brother) and the other believers. None of the apostles were there. In fact, it was possibly just the women, and that is how it happens many times in the church—it is the women who pray and battle in the Spirit for the church.

Herod's end

18 In the morning, there was no small commotion among the soldiers as to what had become of Peter. 19 After Herod had a thorough search made for him and did not find him, he cross-examined the guards and ordered that they be executed. Then Herod went from Judea to Caesarea and stayed there.

The authorities never found Peter after his miraculous escape, but it looks like Herod did not really pursue him. Perhaps Herod did not want the people to know about the security lapse in the prison. For some reason, he stopped persecuting the church and went to Caesarea, where he may have had the opportunity to hear Cornelius' testimony, but he never gave his life to Christ:

20 He had been quarreling with the people of Tyre and Sidon; they now joined together and sought an audience with him. After securing the support of Blastus, a trusted personal servant of the king, they asked for peace, because they depended on the king's country for their food supply.

21 On the appointed day Herod, wearing his royal robes, sat on his throne and delivered a public address to the people. 22 They shouted, "This is the voice of a god, not of a man." 23 Immediately, because Herod did not give praise to God, an angel of the Lord struck him down, and he was eaten by worms and died.

This is clearly presented as God's punishment. The person who persecutes the body of Christ is going to pay. Herod was a proud man; the Lord struck him down because he did not give glory to God.

Status of the church
24 But the word of God continued to spread and flourish.

Here is the same pattern: an event, and then a portrait of the church (a very small one!). In this case, once again, it began with a difficult situation: persecution. James paid with his life, and Peter was saved by a miracle from God. It did not stop the growth of the church, nor its spread to other regions of the empire. We began the chapter with James dead, Peter imprisoned, and Herod triumphant; we finish it with Herod dead, Peter free, and the Word of God triumphant.

15

Paul and Barnabas Sent on Their First Missionary Journey

Acts 12, 13 &14

12:25 *When Barnabas and Saul had finished their mission, they returned from Jerusalem, taking with them John, also called Mark.*

The last time we saw Barnabas and Saul (Acts 11:30), they were taking an offering from Antioch to the church in Jerusalem. They may have been there for James' death and Peter's imprisonment; the exact chronology is not precise.

The church was praying for Peter in John Mark's mother's house (12:12). Barnabas had a keen eye for potential servants in the Lord's work; he would spend time with them and release them into a ministry. He brought Saul to Jerusalem and then went looking for him in Tarsus. Now the two of them took John Mark to Antioch with them. What a beautiful ministry: Introduce believers to the mission field or another culture and mentor them. No wonder they gave him the name Barnabas, which means "Son of consolation" or "Son of encouragement" (Acts 4:36). Could you be a Barnabas for someone?

Barnabas and Saul called and ordained

13:1 Now in the church at Antioch there were prophets and teachers: Barnabas, Simeon called Niger, Lucius of Cyrene, Manaen (who had been brought up with Herod the tetrarch) and Saul. ² While they were worshiping the Lord and fasting, the Holy Spirit said, "Set apart for me Barnabas and Saul for the work to which I have called them."

This was the first recorded missionary call. These leaders reflected the cosmopolitan nature and diversity of Antioch, just as church leadership today should reflect its diversity:

- Barnabas, a Levite from Cyprus.
- Simeon, a Jewish name, but being called "Niger" or "Black" means he was probably from Africa.
- Lucius from Cyrene, in North Africa.
- Manaen, from the upper class, had been raised with Herod.
- Saul, the Pharisee from Tarsus.

The church was also well-organized, with these men recognized as prophets and teachers, two of the five offices that Paul names in Ephesians 4:11. One person can fill two of these offices—or more; Paul was an apostle.

The call came in the context of the church, in a worship service, with the gifts functioning according to God's plan. Furthermore, they were fasting, seeking the Lord, and in his presence. Someone can receive a call from God alone (like Moses and the burning bush), but there is order in the kingdom of God that was very obvious with the Old Testament priesthood, and is still very important today. God operates within the authority of the church.

The Spirit called two men. Although there are cases when someone goes alone, Jesus sent the disciples two by two, and it is the biblical pattern. Saul already knew that his work would be with Gentiles; the Spirit led Barnabas to bring him to Antioch so they could work together.

³ So after they had fasted and prayed, they placed their hands on them and sent them off.

Ordination by a church is as important as the call. A "call" that is not recognized by someone's church should be suspect—someone who claims they do not need to be part of a church is really suspect! It is dangerous (spiritually and physically) to go out on the mission field without that covering. The church in Antioch obeyed the Spirit without question, but they spent time fasting in preparation to pray, lay hands on them, and send them off. What a great encouragement as you face the challenges of the mission field to know you have a body of believers who love you, sent you out, and are praying for you.

Sent by the Holy Spirit

⁴ The two of them, sent on their way by the Holy Spirit, went down to Seleucia and sailed from there to Cyprus.

When the calling and ordination take place in God's order, the Holy Spirit, through the Body of Christ, will send you on your way. If the Holy Spirit sends you, you can be certain he will guide and anoint you and prepare the way. I would hate to go on a mission trip if the Holy Spirit had not sent me!

First, they went down to Seleucia, Antioch's port, about 24 km (15 miles) from the city. Not surprisingly, they first sailed to

Cyprus, Barnabas' birthplace. He already knew the island and its culture.

5 When they arrived at Salamis, they proclaimed the word of God in the Jewish synagogues. John was with them as their helper.

Although Paul's call was to the Gentiles, he always started in the Jewish synagogue. John Mark was not part of the Holy Spirit's call, but now we learn that he accompanied them as an assistant and student.

Paul confronts a false prophet

6 They traveled through the whole island until they came to Paphos. There they met a Jewish sorcerer and false prophet named Bar-Jesus, 7 who was an attendant of the proconsul, Sergius Paulus. The proconsul, an intelligent man, sent for Barnabas and Saul because he wanted to hear the word of God. 8 But Elymas the sorcerer (for that is what his name means) opposed them and tried to turn the proconsul from the faith.

They were probably preaching as they traveled from the east coast to the west coast of Cyprus (about 144 km or 90 miles). So far, everything was going smoothly. There is no mention of signs and wonders—they preached the word, and did not experience much opposition from the Jews. The governor, in Paphos, the provincial capital, was spiritually hungry. It was common for rulers to have a sorcerer or magician advising them; in his case, it was a false prophet. Sergius Paulus had heard of Barnabas and Saul and sent for them. He received the Word with faith, but Elymas, the sorcerer, did not want to lose his position and influence, and opposed them.

What do we learn about Elymas?

- He was Jewish, but not observant; he did not keep the law.
- He was a sorcerer, but also a false prophet. Could it be that many false prophets operate with a spirit of sorcery? They may receive messages, but they are from the evil one.
- His name "Bar-jesus" means "son of salvation" (but he had nothing to do with Jesus Christ).
- Even smart men, like Sergius Paulus, can be deceived by false prophets.
- A false prophet or sorcerer will try to turn the believer away from his faith.

How would Barnabas and Saul respond?

⁹ Then Saul, who was also called Paul, filled with the Holy Spirit, looked straight at Elymas and said, ¹⁰ "You are a child of the devil and an enemy of everything that is right! You are full of all kinds of deceit and trickery. Will you never stop perverting the right ways of the Lord? ¹¹ Now the hand of the Lord is against you. You are going to be blind for a time, not even able to see the light of the sun."

For the first time, Luke called Saul "Paul" (and never called him Saul again), and Paul experienced a special anointing of the Holy Spirit. Similar to Peter and John when they fixed their eyes on the lame man at the Beautiful Gate (Acts 3), Paul fixed his eyes on Elymas, and spoke the truth, inspired by the Spirit:

- He was a child of the devil. He was not only wrong, he was demonized, a servant of Satan.
- He was an enemy of all righteousness. False prophets may look like sheep, but inside they are wolves, and enemies of everything that is right.
- He was full of all kinds of deceit and trickery.

- He perverted the right ways of the Lord. A false prophet may proclaim things supposedly from God or the Bible, but will twist and pervert them.
- Someone had to reveal what he was, and Paul proclaimed that the Lord's hand was now against him. Evil people harm the Lord's work, but God may be waiting for someone like Paul (or you?) to proclaim judgment against them.
- A sign—blindness—will confirm what Paul says. Paul knew what that was like; he experienced it on the road to Damascus.

Paul did not offer him the chance to repent; he will be under God's judgment.

Immediately mist and darkness came over him, and he groped about, seeking someone to lead him by the hand. ¹² When the proconsul saw what had happened, he believed, for he was amazed at the teaching about the Lord.

With great faith, under the anointing of the Spirit, Paul declared blindness, and it happened. We do not know anything else about what happened to Elymas, but it was enough to bring the governor to faith. As we see so many times, the manifestation of God's power confirms the word and results in the person believing and marveling at the Lord.

Nothing is said about how long they stayed there or if they tried to form a church. They continued on their journey.

John Mark leaves them in Pamphylia

¹³ From Paphos, Paul and his companions sailed to Perga in Pamphylia, where John left them to return to Jerusalem. ¹⁴ From Perga they went on to Pisidian Antioch. On the Sabbath they entered the synagogue and sat down. ¹⁵ After the reading from the Law and the Prophets, the leaders of the synagogue sent word to them, saying, "Brothers, if you have a word of exhortation for the people, please speak."

A significant change occurred on Cyprus: Paul took the leading position and, as his name suggests, Barnabas served to support him. That may not have set well with John Mark, and at the first opportunity, he left them to go home to Jerusalem. Sometimes our attempts to bring someone into the ministry are premature or not guided by the Lord. Sadly, the problem with John Mark led to the separation of Paul and Barnabas (Acts 15:36–41), although later he traveled with Paul. Possibly, in God's plan, John Mark spent that time in Jerusalem with Peter, writing the Gospel of Mark.

It was a journey of about 160 km (100 miles) from the coast of Asia (today's Turkey) to Antioch of Pisidia. In accordance with the custom of the Jews, the visitors had the opportunity to share a word in the synagogue:

16 Standing up, Paul motioned with his hand and said: "Fellow Israelites and you Gentiles who worship God, listen to me!

This is Paul's first recorded sermon (verses 17–41), and it follows a pattern similar to Peter's preaching:

- The history of Israel, with an emphasis on God's grace taking the initiative. He focused on David: *God testified concerning him: 'I have found David son of Jesse, a man after my own heart; he will do everything I want him to do.'*
- The ministry of John the Baptist.
- The death and resurrection of Jesus Christ, fulfilling Old Testament prophecies.

- Jesus offers forgiveness of sin if they do not harden their hearts.

It is Christ-centered and biblical. He ends his sermon with this quote from 2 Samuel 7:13–14:

> *⁴¹ "'Look, you scoffers,*
> *wonder and perish,*
> *for I am going to do something in your days*
> *that you would never believe,*
> *even if someone told you.'"*

⁴² As Paul and Barnabas were leaving the synagogue, the people invited them to speak further about these things on the next Sabbath. ⁴³ When the congregation was dismissed, many of the Jews and devout converts to Judaism followed Paul and Barnabas, who talked with them and urged them to continue in the grace of God.

Praise God! They received the Word and invited them back; meanwhile, during the week, Paul and Barnabas continued to share the Word and encouraged them to persevere in God's grace.

⁴⁴ On the next Sabbath almost the whole city gathered to hear the word of the Lord. ⁴⁵ When the Jews saw the crowds, they were filled with jealousy. They began to contradict what Paul was saying and heaped abuse on him.

The news had spread, and practically everyone in the city was there! But the Jews, who had been so open at first, were jealous, and contradicted everything Paul said, *abusing, slandering* (NLT) and *blaspheming* (NASB) him. Can Paul salvage this great opportunity to establish a church?

⁴⁶ Then Paul and Barnabas answered them boldly: "We had to speak the word of God to you first. Since you reject it and do not consider yourselves worthy of eternal life, we now turn to the Gentiles. ⁴⁷ For this is what the Lord has commanded us:

*"'I have made you a light for the Gentiles,
that you may bring salvation to the ends of the earth.'"*

⁴⁸ When the Gentiles heard this, they were glad and honored the word of the Lord; and all who were appointed for eternal life believed.

As so often happened, the Jews had the first opportunity to believe, but they rejected the word, and now Paul and Barnabas addressed the Gentiles, who received the word of salvation with great joy.

Here is a hint of something that has caused much controversy in the church: it speaks of some who "*were appointed* (NLT: *chosen*) *for eternal life.*" That was not everyone, but God prepared these people to receive the Word and believe in Jesus. It is not the purpose of this book to resolve this controversy; we simply have to recognize that the idea of some being destined, appointed, or chosen for salvation exists in the Word, and we can trust the Spirit to open their hearts.

⁴⁹ The word of the Lord spread through the whole region. ⁵⁰ But the Jewish leaders incited the God-fearing women of high standing and the leading men of the city. They stirred up persecution against Paul and Barnabas, and expelled them from their region. ⁵¹ So they shook the dust off their feet as a warning to them and went to Iconium. ⁵² And the disciples were filled with joy and with the Holy Spirit.

Luke ends this portion with a summary of the church there. Paul and Barnabas were very successful, preaching throughout the region and leaving the disciples filled with joy and the Spirit. Those who were not *"appointed for eternal life"* were jealous and had connections with influential people in the city. Once again, Paul and Barnabas were persecuted and driven out of the region, shaking the dust off their feet, according to Jesus' instructions (Lk. 9:5; 10:11).

The journey continues in chapter 14

There is much of interest in Paul's travels, but we will not study them all.

Their experience at Iconium (14:1–7) sounds familiar: They started with the Jews, who rejected them, but *"a multitude"* of Jews and Greeks believed. Here, for the first time, Barnabas was called an apostle. They spent *"considerable time"* there, *"speaking boldly,"* with many signs and wonders. When they became aware of a plot to stone them, they fled to Lystra and Derbe. Good decision!

At Lystra (14:8–20), the healing of a man crippled from birth opened a way for the gospel, but the people called Barnabas "Zeus" and Paul "Hermes," and wanted to offer them sacrifices, as to the gods. In this pagan city, Paul did not speak about the Old Testament, but about the living God of creation. In a dramatic change from worshipping them as gods, *some Jews came from Antioch and Iconium and won the crowd over. They stoned Paul and dragged him outside the city, thinking he was dead* (14:19).

Derbe and the return home

It would be hard for Paul, who was so severely injured they thought he was dead, to walk the 100 km (60 miles) to Derbe, but things were calmer there. We do not know how long they stayed, but from Derbe they revisited the cities where they had left disciples, and then, after almost two years, returned home.

²¹ They preached the gospel in that city and won a large number of disciples. Then they returned to Lystra, Iconium and Antioch, ²² strengthening the disciples and encouraging them to remain true to the faith. "We must go through many hardships to enter the kingdom of God," they said. ²³ Paul and Barnabas appointed elders for them in each church and, with prayer and fasting, committed them to the Lord, in whom they had put their trust. ²⁴ After going through Pisidia, they came into Pamphylia, ²⁵ and when they had preached the word in Perga, they went down to Attalia.

This is an important part of follow-up. From their own experience, they could talk about the "many difficulties" we go through to enter the kingdom—quite possibly, these new believers were already experiencing them. New disciples need to be strengthened and encouraged to persevere in faith. The love shown by Paul and Barnabas in returning to see them meant much, as well as their words of encouragement and prayers. That personal touch is essential in follow-up, whether in person or online. Jesus commanded us to "make disciples," not "converts." We have infinitely more resources than Paul did to strengthen and encourage young believers.

They not only encouraged the brothers, they formed churches with elders. Even though they had only been saved for a few months, it would already be apparent who was persevering and had the heart to guide the church. It is difficult to leave a young church, knowing that these elders would experience many difficulties, but they entrusted them to the Lord, with their faith expressed in prayer and fasting—Jesus will take care of them. Paul's goal in his missionary work was not fame or masses of converts, but to establish churches, bodies of Jesus Christ, in every place. He would forever be their "spiritual father" and provide spiritual covering for these churches.

26 From Attalia they sailed back to Antioch, where they had been committed to the grace of God for the work they had now completed. 27 On arriving there, they gathered the church together and reported all that God had done through them and how he had opened a door of faith to the Gentiles. 28 And they stayed there a long time with the disciples.

They had been "commended to the grace of God" months before, when they left their church in Antioch. They had been through *"many difficulties,"* but God had been faithful, and they returned with many testimonies to share with a church hungry for news about them. Today we have connections with everyone via WhatsApp or other online applications, but back then, months could go by with no news. No wonder they stayed there a long time—to rest, minister to the church, and be refreshed in the Lord.

16

The Jerusalem Council

Acts 15:1–35

¹*Certain people came down from Judea to Antioch and were teaching the believers: "Unless you are circumcised, according to the custom taught by Moses, you cannot be saved."*

This kind of problem comes with rapid church growth. In this case, it was the inclusion of Gentiles and other cultures. We noted that the church in Antioch had Greek-speakers and people from various provinces, and not all of them were keeping the Old Testament Law. The situation was very different in Jerusalem, where Jewish customs and the Law still held sway.

Over the centuries, the church has faced many theological issues and disagreements on Christian conduct. This chapter provides a model of how to solve them. The goal is to maintain unity—for several centuries the church was quite successful at that. Today, we have lost the concept of Christ's delegated authority to apostles who oversee the church. If there is disagreement, the church often divides, a new denomination or council is formed, or they proclaim themselves "independent" of all ecclesiastical authority. In this case, it would have resulted in one church for the circumcised (Jewish) and another for the non-circumcised (Gentile).

The direction of the rest of Acts—and church history—will be decided here. Will it always be a Jerusalem-based Jewish sect that recognizes Jesus as its messiah? Or will it continue to spread throughout the empire to Rome, the capital?

² This brought Paul and Barnabas into sharp dispute and debate with them.

The Judean brothers entered another church's territory without respecting the authority of its leadership. Later, Paul wrote about someone who tried to enforce Jewish law: *The one who is throwing you into confusion, whoever that may be, will have to pay the penalty* (Gal. 5:10).

It is possible that Paul wrote Galatians reflecting on this situation:

When Cephas came to Antioch, I opposed him to his face, because he stood condemned. For before certain men came from James, he used to eat with the Gentiles. But when they arrived, he began to draw back and separate himself from the Gentiles because he was afraid of those who belonged to the circumcision group. The other Jews joined him in his hypocrisy, so that by their hypocrisy even Barnabas was led astray.

When I saw that they were not acting in line with the truth of the gospel, I said to Cephas in front of them all, "You are a Jew, yet you live like a Gentile and not like a Jew. How is it, then, that you force Gentiles to follow Jewish customs?

"We who are Jews by birth and not sinful Gentiles know that a person is not justified by the works of the law, but by faith in Jesus Christ. So we, too, have put our faith in Christ Jesus that we may be justified by faith in Christ and not by the works of the law,

because by the works of the law no one will be justified (Gal. 2:11–16).

Paul and Barnabas had recently returned from their mission trip. They were leaders in the church and had seen many Gentiles receive the Gospel. Paul was a stubborn man, a trait God used to preserve the sound doctrine of justification by faith. He was not about to give in on this point, which is the very foundation of the Gospel. It came up again in the Reformation, when many believers (like Martin Luther) left the Catholic Church. Is faith in Christ sufficient for salvation? Or is it Christ plus circumcision, the Law, or some other work? All the other world religions require something on our part to reach God. It is a constant temptation for Christians today as well. They may not say it explicitly, but in their practice and teachings, many add some requirement to be a true Christian.

So Paul and Barnabas were appointed, along with some other believers, to go up to Jerusalem to see the apostles and elders about this question.

It could be tempting to separate from Jerusalem and send the "Judaizers" back home, but they decided to do the right thing, trust God, and appeal to the apostles and elders of the mother church.

³ The church sent them on their way, and as they traveled through Phoenicia and Samaria, they told how the Gentiles had been converted. This news made all the believers very glad. ⁴ When they came to Jerusalem, they were welcomed by the church and the apostles and elders, to whom they reported everything God had done through them.

Again, just as on their mission trip, they were sent by the church, probably with prayer and fasting. On the way they shared what

God had done among the Gentiles, and arrived in Jerusalem to a warm welcome, encouraged by the joy with which their testimonies had been received.

5 Then some of the believers who belonged to the party of the Pharisees stood up and said, "The Gentiles must be circumcised and required to keep the law of Moses."

Not surprisingly, Pharisees who had received Christ firmly held to the importance of circumcision and obedience to the Law.

6 The apostles and elders met to consider this question. They held the authority to determine what would be church doctrine.

7 After much discussion, Peter got up and addressed them: "Brothers, you know that some time ago God made a choice among you that the Gentiles might hear from my lips the message of the gospel and believe. 8 God, who knows the heart, showed that he accepted them by giving the Holy Spirit to them, just as he did to us. 9 He did not discriminate between us and them, for he purified their hearts by faith. 10 Now then, why do you try to test God by putting on the necks of Gentiles a yoke that neither we nor our ancestors have been able to bear? 11 No! We believe it is through the grace of our Lord Jesus that we are saved, just as they are."

Peter immediately put God in charge. It was God who chose Peter, knows the human heart, and was responsible for the change in Peter's attitude toward the Gentiles. To not accept his sovereign work is to test (NLT: *challenge*) God. For Peter, the vision he had in Joppa (Acts 9) and the miraculous conversion of Cornelius and his family were confirmations not only of the inclusion of the Gentiles but also of a change in the laws of the Old Testament (in that case, regarding food). On that basis, Peter suggested several points—and made his last appearance in this book!

- It was God who accepted them and confirmed it with the gift of the Holy Spirit.
- God makes no distinction between Jew and Gentile.
- Our hearts are cleansed by faith; what matters is internal, not external (like circumcision).
- Adding something that God has not commanded tests or provokes him.
- Legalism is like a yoke on the believer's neck.
- Peter was honest and acknowledged that neither they nor their ancestors could bear the requirements of the Law.
- Salvation is by the grace of Jesus Christ.

[12] The whole assembly became silent as they listened to Barnabas and Paul telling about the signs and wonders God had done among the Gentiles through them.

Possibly Luke named Barnabas first because he was better known in Jerusalem and had a less complicated history than Paul. The case they present was not theological, but a testimony of the signs and wonders God did among the Gentiles to confirm his acceptance of them. Paul would present the theological argument in his letters, such as Ephesians 3:2–6, Colossians 1:26–27, and Romans 16:25–27.

To end the presentations, James, Jesus' brother and head of the church in Jerusalem, spoke.

[13] When they finished, James spoke up. "Brothers," he said, "listen to me. [14] Simon has described to us how God first intervened to choose a people for his name from the Gentiles. [15] The words of the prophets are in agreement with this, as it is written:

> ¹⁶ *"'After this I will return*
> *and rebuild David's fallen tent.*
> *Its ruins I will rebuild,*
> *and I will restore it,*
> ¹⁷ *that the rest of mankind may seek the Lord,*
> *even all the Gentiles who bear my name,*
> *says the Lord, who does these things'—*
> ¹⁸ *things known from long ago.*

¹⁹ *"It is my judgment, therefore, that we should not make it difficult for the Gentiles who are turning to God. ²⁰ Instead we should write to them, telling them to abstain from food polluted by idols, from sexual immorality, from the meat of strangled animals and from blood. ²¹ For the law of Moses has been preached in every city from the earliest times and is read in the synagogues on every Sabbath."*

James honored Peter's vision and testimony, stating that it was God's purpose from the beginning to include the Gentiles. He quoted prophecy (Amos 9:11–12) to support that, and then, with his authority, declared what he believed should be the conclusion of the matter:

- Jews are not released from obeying the law (that would come later), but a converted Gentile does not have to submit to it.
- They should not make it difficult for Gentiles, imposing unnecessary burdens or putting obstacles on those who accept Christ. It is good advice for our evangelization today.
- They must refrain from three things:
  - Food contaminated by idols.
  - Sexual immorality.
  - The meat of strangled animals and blood.

²² Then the apostles and elders, with the whole church, decided to choose some of their own men and send them to Antioch with Paul and Barnabas. They chose Judas (called Barsabbas) and Silas, men who were leaders among the believers.

The decision was not only for the apostles and elders, but for the whole church. It would not be enough to send a letter with Paul and Barnabas. They wanted to send two brothers with them. Luke introduces Silas, who would play an important part in the ministries of Paul and Peter.

²³ With them they sent the following letter:

The apostles and elders, your brothers,

To the Gentile believers in Antioch, Syria and Cilicia:

Greetings.

²⁴ We have heard that some went out from us without our authorization and disturbed you, troubling your minds by what they said. ²⁵ So we all agreed to choose some men and send them to you with our dear friends Barnabas and Paul— ²⁶ men who have risked their lives for the name of our Lord Jesus Christ. ²⁷ Therefore we are sending Judas and Silas to confirm by word of mouth what we are writing. ²⁸ It seemed good to the Holy Spirit and to us not to burden you with anything beyond the following requirements: ²⁹ You are to abstain from food sacrificed to idols, from blood, from the meat of strangled animals and from sexual immorality. You will do well to avoid these things.

Farewell.

The letter was addressed to Gentile brothers in three regions (it is not necessarily a universal letter of church doctrine). It came from the apostles and elders in Jerusalem—calling them "brothers" in the greeting was an important sign of their acceptance.

- They acknowledged that the men who went to Antioch were from the Jerusalem church, but did not have their authorization. A member of the church does not have the right to go and preach what they want somewhere else; they must go with the permission of the church leadership.

- They do not want to disturb or alarm the brothers; we should beware of those who might do so.

- They honor the church leaders in Antioch (Paul and Barnabas), calling them "*dear friends*" (NASB: *beloved*) who "*have risked their lives for the name of our Lord Jesus Christ.*"

- After discussing the matter, they believed they had discerned the Spirit's mind and agreed to the three standards. They did not want to impose additional burdens on them.

[30] So the men were sent off and went down to Antioch, where they gathered the church together and delivered the letter. [31] The people read it and were glad for its encouraging message. [32] Judas and Silas, who themselves were prophets, said much to encourage and strengthen the believers. [33] After spending some time there, they were sent off by the believers with the blessing of peace to return to those who had sent them. [34] But Silas decided to remain there. [35] But Paul and Barnabas remained in Antioch, where they and many others taught and preached the word of the Lord.

Now we learn that the two brothers sent from Jerusalem, Judas and Silas, were prophets. They not only delivered the letter but spoke *"much"* (NASB: *with a lengthy message*) to encourage and strengthen the church. The portion concludes with the "status of the church" that we have seen frequently in Acts. A problem arose, the church confronted it, and now peace and blessing return to the church.

17

Paul Starts His Second Voyage with a New Partner

Acts 15:36–16:5

³⁶ Some time later Paul said to Barnabas, "Let us go back and visit the believers in all the towns where we preached the word of the Lord and see how they are doing."

A fter a break at home in Antioch (15:35), Paul suggested something that had to be born of the Holy Spirit, it is so close to God's heart: A follow-up to encourage the elders and churches they planted on their first journey. Without the social media we have today, letters would be the only way to stay in touch aside from a personal visit.

Conflict between Paul and Barnabas

³⁷ Barnabas wanted to take John, also called Mark, with them, ³⁸ but Paul did not think it wise to take him, because he had deserted them in Pamphylia and had not continued with them in the work.

John Mark was traveling between Antioch and Jerusalem, where he was helping Peter. His cousin Barnabas saw his gifts and potential. He was always ready to encourage others, and wanted to give John Mark another opportunity, even though he had abandoned them, but Paul did not think it was wise. It is a delicate balance: We want to offer forgiveness, mercy, grace, and compassion—that was Barnabas' character. However, there are also practical issues of conducting a mission when someone you are counting on abruptly leaves. In ministry, we need boundaries with people who are immature emotionally, spiritually, or personally.

³⁹ *They had such a sharp disagreement that they parted company.*

As brothers in Christ, through prayer and fasting, we hope to reach an agreement. Nevertheless, even among Christians, there are conflicts, and the only solution may be to separate (that does not apply to marriage, which is a covenant made before God!). Sometimes we realize that God has different plans for two people who have been working together, and we amicably separate. That can happen with a church and a pastor as well. We can spend a lot of energy trying to maintain a situation when God is telling us to make a change.

Barnabas took Mark and sailed for Cyprus, ⁴⁰ but Paul chose Silas and left, commended by the believers to the grace of the Lord. ⁴¹ He went through Syria and Cilicia, strengthening the churches.

Barnabas returned to his homeland. Unfortunately, it does not say that the church entrusted him to the Lord's grace, and we know nothing more about him—he disappears from the history of the church. Hopefully, Barnabas was still useful to the Lord—a situation like this can discourage someone until they leave the ministry or even their faith. Tradition holds that he founded the

Cypriot Orthodox Church and was eventually martyred. Mark flourished in his ministry and later accompanied Paul (2 Tim. 4:11, Philemon 1:24).

Silas, one of the elders sent from Jerusalem with the council's letter, left with Paul and became a faithful helper to him. While the Holy Spirit chose Paul and Barnabas (12:1), Paul chose Silas. It would seem better to have the Spirit choose, but it may be an apostle's right to make that decision. The goal was to *"visit the believers in all the towns"* where Paul and Barnabas preached, but Paul left Cyprus to Barnabas.

16:1 Paul came to Derbe and then to Lystra, where a disciple named Timothy lived, whose mother was Jewish and a believer but whose father was a Greek. 2 The believers at Lystra and Iconium spoke well of him. 3 Paul wanted to take him along on the journey, so he circumcised him because of the Jews who lived in that area, for they all knew that his father was a Greek. 4 As they traveled from town to town, they delivered the decisions reached by the apostles and elders in Jerusalem for the people to obey.

Since his first visit to Lystra, a young man had risen up and distinguished himself in the ministry. Paul decided to take him on this mission trip, perhaps remembering how Barnabas took him under his wing—another example of an apostle or Christian leader noticing the potential in a young man and inviting him to minister together. Timothy would be one of Paul's most important disciples.

One purpose of Paul's trip was to share the decision of the Jerusalem council with these churches, which stated that a Gentile Christian does not have to be circumcised. Timothy was in a hard place: He had a Gentile father, but a Jewish mother, and the Jews still believed a Jew needed to be circumcised. It can seem like a contradiction to the ruling of the Jerusalem Council, but in order not to offend them, Paul circumcised him.

⁵ So the churches were strengthened in the faith and grew daily in numbers.

This portion includes the circumcision issue, its resolution in Jerusalem, and communicating that decision to the churches. Characteristically, Luke ends with a summary of the state of the church. Though brief, it is very positive. With the issue of the Gentiles clarified, the churches experienced two things God wants for every church: to be strengthened in the faith (grow spiritually) and to grow in number every day. By its nature, the body of Jesus grows. If it is not growing, something is wrong.

18

What to do When You Find Yourself in a Dungeon

Acts 16:6–40

If you want to be useful to the Lord, there is a simple pattern we have seen in Acts: be available, listen to his voice, and obey what he says. Paul followed that here, walking as Christ walked. This passage reminds me of a fight, of a boxing match. Paul entered the ring well prepared, left bloodied and bruised, but, as usual, ended victorious through God's grace.

Prepare for the work that God has for you

First, in the comfort of your home and church, wait on the Lord to discern his will:

⁶ Paul and his companions traveled throughout the region of Phrygia and Galatia, having been kept by the Holy Spirit from preaching the word in the province of Asia. ⁷ When they came to the border of Mysia, they tried to enter Bithynia, but the Spirit of Jesus would not allow them to.

Paul knocked on doors and found them closed. He was not in sin; I am sure he had prayed and was aware of the great need in Asia (what is now Turkey). Paul was available and had a burning desire to preach the gospel throughout the world. There is a saying: "You can't steer a parked car." Sometimes, we have to tentatively start moving and knock on several doors before one opens. But there are also times when we have to pray and wait. If you feel unsure, it may be best to stay where you are until you receive confirmation to move.

How did the Spirit keep them from preaching in Asia? How did he "*not allow*" them to preach in Bithynia? We do not know. It could be circumstances, the advice of a Christian brother, or an inner voice. In your life, has the Spirit ever forbidden you to do something, or not allowed something? In my experience, it starts with an uneasiness, almost a dread. Something that in itself is good suddenly fills you with fear. Something you wanted to do is suddenly the last thing you want to do.

At that point, you have to discern:

- Is it the devil's opposition? Do you have to battle him? Satan can also stop you. Paul wrote in 1 Thessalonians 2:18: *For we wanted to come to you—certainly I, Paul, did, again and again—but Satan blocked our way.*
- Is the Lord testing you, or teaching you perseverance and faith?
- Or is it a simple "no" from God?

Some stubborn people insist on going ahead and ignore the Spirit's leading, but it is very dangerous to go where he has forbidden you to enter. I have heard stories of missionaries who were banned from entering a country, and it turns out there was a coup d'état, and they would have been in great danger. There are many stories of someone who believes that God does not want them to board a flight, and the plane crashed. Learn to listen to the tender voice of the Spirit.

⁸ So they passed by Mysia and went down to Troas. ⁹ During the night Paul had a vision of a man of Macedonia standing and begging him, "Come over to Macedonia and help us." ¹⁰ After Paul had seen the vision, we got ready at once to leave for Macedonia, concluding that God had called us to preach the gospel to them.

A night vision is similar to a dream, but more impressive and more memorable. Paul was available; now he received a clear call to go to Macedonia, and immediately obeyed. Until now, he had been with his brothers, waiting on the Lord. We can have beautiful times of communion with God at home or in the loving fellowship of the brothers, but after that great Sunday service, on Monday we have to go back to work or school, or deal with problems at home. Paul and his companions (Silas, Timothy, and Luke) were ready for the second step.

Entering the battlefield

Now they started their mission, ready to invade the devil's territory and proclaim the good news. However, like Jesus Christ, they were on a path that led to suffering.

¹¹ From Troas we put out to sea and sailed straight for Samothrace, and the next day we went on to Neapolis. ¹² From there we traveled to Philippi, a Roman colony and the leading city of that district of Macedonia. And we stayed there several days.

They crossed the Aegean Sea to Macedonia by boat, first to Samothrace (a small, mountainous island) and the next day to Neapolis. As usual, Paul first went to the principal city of the province; from there, they evangelized the other districts.

Philippi was a prosperous, pagan city with gold and silver mines nearby. An arch at the entrance to the city announced that unknown religions were forbidden. It was a very Roman city, with many retired Roman soldiers. There was no synagogue, and possibly no Jews.

When they arrived, they did not immediately start evangelizing, but spent a few days in prayer, possibly fasting, getting to know the city and what principalities and powers were operating in it. Obedient to the prohibition to evangelize within the city, they learned of a prayer meeting by the river, and waited for Saturday to join them:

13 On the Sabbath we went outside the city gate to the river, where we expected to find a place of prayer. We sat down and began to speak to the women who had gathered there.

Then, as now, it is often the women who come together to pray. It was a small beginning, but we will see it was enough to attract the enemy's attention.

You might question why God called them to Macedonia:

- It does not seem like a very fertile field.
- There is no synagogue.
- Paul could not preach in the forum.
- In their first meeting there are only a few women.
- There are no miracles or deliverances.

However, we start with what the Lord gives us, and many miracles and large numbers are not always the sign of success. In the first round, Christ won a soul:

14 One of those listening was a woman from the city of Thyatira named Lydia, a dealer in purple cloth. She was a worshiper of God. The Lord opened her heart to respond to Paul's message.

Purple cloth was expensive and was worn as a token of nobility or royalty. Thyatira, one of the seven churches that received letters in Revelation, was a city in the interior of Asia, about 600 km (372 miles) from Philippi, famous for its dyeing facilities and a center of the purple cloth trade, which Lydia came to Philippi to sell. She was a foreigner, relatively wealthy, and possibly more knowledgeable about Judaism than the others.

We have to do our part and announce the Word, but the Lord opens the hearts to listen and respond to the message. We pray that God would open the hearts of co-workers, friends, and family.

¹⁵ *When she and the members of her household were baptized, she invited us to her home. "If you consider me a believer in the Lord," she said, "come and stay at my house." And she persuaded us.*

Many times, a church starts with a family, which in the past could include many people. Of the women by the river, only Lydia accepted the Lord; she shared the word with her family (it never mentions a husband). As a merchant, she had a large and comfortable house. The Lord supplied the place, and the brothers stayed there, in obedience to Jesus' instructions to his disciples (Lk. 10:7).

The battle intensifies: A clash of kingdoms
When we do the Lord's work and the Holy Spirit moves with conversions and miracles, the devil and his demons will resist:

¹⁶ *Once when we were going to the place of prayer, we were met by a female slave who had a spirit by which she predicted the future. She earned a great deal of money for her owners by fortune-telling. ¹⁷ She followed Paul and the rest of us, shouting,*

"These men are servants of the Most High God, who are telling you the way to be saved."

Often, there will be opposition on the way to the church or to prayer: an argument with the wife, problems with the children, or a car that won't start. This girl was a slave; she had masters, and they were probably abusing her. Often in Jesus' ministry, the demonized person recognized him as the Son of God—much more than religious people did! Demons recognize God's true servants and fear them, but for some reason, they also draw attention to them. Don't be concerned if demons manifest in your presence; it is a confirmation that you are filled with the Holy Spirit.

In the Greek, this spirit is called a python spirit. Spirits have names, and this is a very ugly one. He is around today, sometimes in the church, where he masquerades as a spirit of prophecy. Divination is predicting the future; there may be some revelation of future events, but, as always with the devil, it is mixed with lies.

Paul did not want that kind of testimony. First, it was against the law to evangelize within the city, and he did not want to attract attention. Moreover, people paid for the girl's services; she made a lot of money for her masters, and Paul did not want problems with them.

The second round: Christ wins one more
[18] She kept this up for many days. Finally Paul became so annoyed that he turned around and said to the spirit, "In the name of Jesus Christ I command you to come out of her!" At that moment the spirit left her.

Why did Paul wait so long to rebuke the spirit? Possibly, he already knew that there would be ugly consequences from her masters. Whether it is a gang of drug traffickers, prostitutes, or people with another vice, it is always dangerous when money is involved. She followed them *"many days,"* until Paul was finally fed up and rebuked the spirit with authority, in the name of Jesus. You have that same power and authority to rebuke unclean spirits, but it is not something we do lightly—you must be spiritually prepared, and ready for the consequences.

Our tendency is to think that when we walk like Christ in God's power, there will be blessings and everything will be fine, but that is not always the case. You may love the Lord and be walking in obedience to him, but suddenly, all hell has broken loose. It does not necessarily mean that you are in sin or that God is angry with you.

Round three: They approach the cross, whipped by the enemy

[19] When her owners realized that their hope of making money was gone, they seized Paul and Silas and dragged them into the marketplace to face the authorities. [20] They brought them before the magistrates and said, "These men are Jews, and are throwing our city into an uproar [21] by advocating customs unlawful for us Romans to accept or practice."

Her masters had no interest in her well-being; they were just thinking about the money and their pleasure abusing her. In addition to questions of race, culture, religion, and the economy, Paul and his companions had violated the prohibition on introducing new beliefs to the city.

[22] The crowd joined in the attack against Paul and Silas, and the magistrates ordered them to be stripped and beaten with rods.

We do not know what happened to Timothy and Luke, but there, in front of everyone, were the great apostle and Silas, naked.

Being whipped with rods was brutal. They whipped the entire body, including the feet, hoping to break those bones. The Jews had a limit of thirty-nine lashes, but the Romans had no limit. Many died from a beating with rods.

[23] After they had been severely flogged, they were thrown into prison, and the jailer was commanded to guard them carefully. [24] When he received these orders, he put them in the inner cell and fastened their feet in the stocks.

They were bloody, naked, and in the maximum security inner cell (or dungeon), with their feet in the stocks. They were in a Roman province, but were foreigners, and without a lawyer. The situation is dire. Why did this happen? Where is God? What did they do wrong? Had they sinned? No! In this world, there are times when we are beaten with rods—emotionally and spiritually—and it seems that the enemy has won the battle. There is no hope. Paul was ready to die. Years later, he wrote to the church at Philippi:

For to me, to live is Christ and to die is gain. If I am to go on living in the body, this will mean fruitful labor for me. Yet what shall I choose? I do not know! I am torn between the two: I desire to depart and be with Christ, which is better by far; but it is more necessary for you that I remain in the body (Phil. 1:21–24).

Do you feel like you are in a dungeon? Bound up by the enemy? Captive of some sin? Are you going through some tough circumstances? You may not see any way out. There is only darkness. Your feet are in the stocks. Victory seems impossible. But is your circumstance worse than that of Paul and Silas? I don't think so. What hope is there? What can you do?

The man of God rises for the fourth round

25 About midnight Paul and Silas were praying and singing hymns to God, and the other prisoners were listening to them.

When there is nothing else you can do, praise God. There is power in praise. We worship God not only because it feels good and the music is nice—the devil flees from our praises. You may not have a Bible, but you can always pray and worship. At midnight, Paul and Silas were singing praises to God. In the darkest hour, praise God. With a broken heart, praise God. Sing to the Lord. In the shower, praise God. What if the neighbors hear you? Trust God to use your testimony. Were they declaring their release? Were they asking for freedom for the other prisoners? Did they declare a major earthquake? I don't think so. They probably asked God for a miracle, but then entrusted their lives to him and began to worship.

Praise releases a great victory for God

26 Suddenly there was such a violent earthquake that the foundations of the prison were shaken. At once all the prison doors flew open, and everyone's chains came loose.

When Christ died on the cross, the devil thought he had defeated the Son of God. Jesus was in the grave, dead. Paul was in the dungeon, almost dead, but God always has the last word.

When Jesus rose, *There was a violent earthquake, for an angel of the Lord came down from heaven and, going to the tomb, rolled back the stone and sat on it* (Matt. 28:2). Now there was another great earthquake.

We do not have to know how God is going to do it; in this case, he went far beyond their expectations. Do you think God can make the earth quake? Of course he can! There is nothing difficult for him! He can shake the foundations of your home, your town, and your country. He can open doors for you and break all the chains in your life.

When God blesses you, your family and everyone often benefit: all the doors opened and all the prisoners' chains came loose.

27 The jailer woke up, and when he saw the prison doors open, he drew his sword and was about to kill himself because he thought the prisoners had escaped. 28 But Paul shouted, "Don't harm yourself! We are all here!"

God opened the doors and broke their chains. They could escape and flee the city, but they stayed inside, and God did something impressive in the other prisoners, too—none of them fled. Perhaps they were overwhelmed with God's power and glory, and the praises of Paul and Silas touched their hearts. Paul rose up in authority: God came to save, not to kill. Paul knows that God loves the jailer.

Another round, at night, and a family won for Christ

29 The jailer called for lights, rushed in and fell trembling before Paul and Silas. 30 He then brought them out and asked, "Sirs, what must I do to be saved?"

When you have God's favor, powerful people will come trembling and bow down at your feet, seeking God's blessing. Do you believe God can work in your life in such a way that others see his power and ask you how to be saved?

31 They replied, "Believe in the Lord Jesus, and you will be saved— you and your household."

Salvation is a matter of faith and a relationship with Jesus Christ. This verse has given rise to a common belief that the salvation of your whole house is promised when you accept Jesus. It is God's will, and many times it does happen as a result of your testimony, but it is not automatic. Each person needs faith and has to make that decision; your faith cannot save another person. You can pray for him in faith and testify in faith, but he has to make his own decision.

32 Then they spoke the word of the Lord to him and to all the others in his house. 33 At that hour of the night the jailer took them and washed their wounds; then immediately he and all his household were baptized. 34 The jailer brought them into his house and set a meal before them; he was filled with joy because he had come to believe in God—he and his whole household.

It might have been one in the morning. No matter. We do not know what happened to the other prisoners. Paul and Silas were covered in blood and seriously injured, but they spoke the Word of God to everyone in the house. Then the jailer washed their wounds, and, perhaps in the same place, the jailer and his family were baptized. Again, we see the importance of baptism; they did not wait for the morning or a service with the other believers. Maybe God healed Paul and Silas, and they all ate. God filled that house with joy.

The end of the story: expelled from the city
35 When it was daylight, the magistrates sent their officers to the jailer with the order: "Release those men." 36 The jailer told Paul, "The magistrates have ordered that you and Silas be released. Now you can leave. Go in peace."

37 But Paul said to the officers: "They beat us publicly without a trial, even though we are Roman citizens, and threw us into prison. And now do they want to get rid of us quietly? No! Let them come themselves and escort us out."

They did not flee through the open prison doors, and now the magistrates offered them their freedom. Again, it seems that God was moving in their favor. The jailer was happy to communicate that decision, but Paul says no, they need to be aware that both Paul and Silas were Roman citizens—it was illegal to beat a Roman citizen with rods or throw them in jail without a sentence. Citizenship was valuable and hard to obtain, but God had prepared that blessing for them. It is not wrong to claim your rights before the law.

38 The officers reported this to the magistrates, and when they heard that Paul and Silas were Roman citizens, they were alarmed. 39 They came to appease them and escorted them from the prison, requesting them to leave the city. 40 After Paul and Silas came out of the prison, they went to Lydia's house, where they met with the brothers and sisters and encouraged them. Then they left.

Now the magistrates were afraid; they asked the brothers to come out. They had a final worship service and left town. What an introduction to Macedonia!

Paul and Silas almost died. They left two families and some prisoners in Philippi to establish a church. At first, it seemed like a defeat, a great victory for the devil, but God is faithful, and he was glorified in an awe-inspiring way. It does not matter where you are or what is happening in your life. Praise God. He can move mountains, break chains, and open prison doors.

19

The Gospel Comes to Ephesus

Acts 18:24–19:12

Ephesus was an important, prosperous, commercial center of the Roman Empire, in what was then called Asia (today's Turkey). Despite a significant Jewish population, it was a very pagan city. The temple to Diana was one of the Seven Wonders of the Ancient World.

The Gospel arrives in Ephesus

Paul had briefly stopped in the city and met some Jews, but left, saying he would return if it were God's will. A missionary we meet here for the first time planted the church (Acts 18:24–28):

Meanwhile a Jew named Apollos, a native of Alexandria, came to Ephesus. He was a learned man, with a thorough knowledge of the Scriptures. He had been instructed in the way of the Lord, and he spoke with great fervor and taught about Jesus accurately, though he knew only the baptism of John. He began to speak boldly in the synagogue. When Priscilla and Aquila heard him, they invited him to their home and explained to him the way of God more adequately.

The man God used

God usually sends an anointed man to start a church. We have read about the work of Philip, Barnabas, and Paul. Apollos was a native of Alexandria, Egypt, one of the most important cities in the Roman Empire. He was:

- A Jew.
- A learned man.
- Thoroughly knowledgeable of the Scriptures (AMP: *well versed and mighty in the Scriptures*).
- Instructed in the way of the Lord.
- A fervent speaker. Literally (NASB): *fervent in spirit,* AMP*: burning with spiritual zeal.*

What a combination! His Jewish faith gave him a solid foundation, and he was well educated, particularly in the Scriptures (the Old Testament at that time). Too often, I have seen theological study rob someone of their zeal and fervor, but not Apollos. He became Paul's co-worker and played an important role in the development of the church in Corinth. On what appears to be his first missionary journey, the Lord sent him to Ephesus, where he went to the synagogue and boldly spoke about the Messiah. We are told he taught accurately about Jesus. This sounds great – but there was a problem.

The danger of limited knowledge

God can powerfully use someone with limited knowledge. He has done so many times. Apollos was a highly educated man who loved the Scriptures. Many highly educated people may know the Scriptures, but lack complete knowledge of the Lord's ways. Many of them are zealous, fervent, and sincere. Nevertheless, they may be sincerely wrong. The church is growing so fast in many areas that there is no time for Bible school, let alone the funds to pay for it. I have noticed an appalling ignorance of church history and the Bible—and how to interpret it—among many church leaders. Perhaps they have a good excuse for their ignorance, yet with such widespread access to the internet and more resources to train leaders than ever before, there are many opportunities to learn.

We cannot blame Apollos for what happened in Ephesus. He did his best with what he knew, which was only John's baptism—a baptism of repentance. He did not know about the baptism Jesus had commanded, of identification with his death and resurrection, or the baptism in the Holy Spirit. Perhaps Apollos heard the Gospel from someone who came to Alexandria, had listened to Jesus and been baptized by John, but left Jerusalem before Pentecost.

Be teachable

More serious than lack of knowledge is an unteachable spirit—a prideful person who is not open to receiving the truth. Thank God, that was not the case with Apollos. God put a couple in his path who took him aside, invited him to their home, and explained the Gospel to him more fully. We are desperately in need of people like Priscilla and Aquila today, who have the love, tenderness, and willingness to pour into the lives of young leaders. Inviting someone to your home shows genuine care. If they need correction, it is always better to take them aside— public correction usually results in defensiveness and is rarely effective. Could God use you (perhaps with your spouse?) to more fully explain the Lord's ways to a young minister?

Apollos sent to Corinth

When Apollos wanted to go to Achaia (Corinth), the brothers and sisters encouraged him and wrote to the disciples there to welcome him. When he arrived, he was a great help to those who by grace had believed. For he vigorously refuted his Jewish opponents in public debate, proving from the Scriptures that Jesus was the Messiah.

One way the church grew so rapidly in the first century was by sending evangelists to other cities to spread the Gospel. Apollos felt called to Corinth, and the brothers in Ephesus encouraged him on his way. God still calls many to go out on "mission trips." It is important to send someone out with a proper recommendation (Such as an Email or a letter) and to ensure that anyone coming to minister in your church comes with the recommendation of a respected pastor or leader.

Apollos was a fast learner and was well equipped to prove the truth about Jesus from the Scriptures. We need to study and prepare ourselves to carefully use the Scriptures to defend our message. Sadly, cult group members often seem better equipped to use the Scriptures for their purposes than we are. It is God's Word, not yours, which has the power to convict and transform. Though we want to be sensitive and not belligerent, there are times to publicly refute the errors of other doctrines—and even do it vigorously, as though you are convinced it is the truth. After all, God needs warriors, not wimps.

Have you known the blessings of receiving someone like Apollos? I pray that you may be of great help to whoever God sends you to. Is there some area in which you, like Apollos, may lack knowledge? Are you open to being taught? What can you do to begin to remedy that lack?

Apollos did his best and laid the foundation for the church, but several key pieces were missing, so God sent another man to fill in those gaps. The church was about to explode, and Paul's arrival provided the needed spark.

Paul arrives in Ephesus

While Apollos was at Corinth, Paul took the road through the interior and arrived at Ephesus. There he found some disciples (19:1).

Paul had not met Apollos and was unaware of his ministry there, but he did find the fruit of his labors—a small group of disciples. Oddly, Paul immediately sensed that something was wrong. We already know there was a problem with their baptism, but now we learn of another problem:

²Paul asked them, "Did you receive the Holy Spirit when you believed?" They answered, "No, we have not even heard that there is a Holy Spirit." ³ So Paul asked, "Then what baptism did you receive?" "John's baptism," they replied.

Believers without the Holy Spirit?

The Lord may have revealed it to him, but most likely Paul noticed something lacking among these disciples: There was no power, no manifestations of the Holy Spirit. He expected that when you believe in Jesus, you receive the Spirit. That was usually the case in Acts: Someone would accept Jesus, be baptized in water, and at the same time be baptized in the Spirit, usually accompanied by speaking in tongues. However, that was not always the case, as we see now in Ephesus. Before he could do any further ministry, Paul's priority was correcting this.

Paul was not pointing fingers or questioning their spirituality. He knew the fullness of the Spirit was essential for the Christian life, and he would do whatever it took to make sure these disciples received it. Without the Spirit's presence, he could not build a church. Here is a clear biblical case (and not the only one) where sincere believers in Jesus had not received the Spirit. Obviously, for some, it is going to be a second experience. How about you? Did you receive the Holy Spirit when you believed? If you are not sure, are you open to whatever the Lord might do to give you that necessary power?

Here, the issue was simple ignorance: They had never even heard there was a Holy Spirit. That is true in some churches, which barely talk about the Spirit. Now, as then, some people do not know about the Spirit, or his role in our lives.

The connection of water and Spirit baptism

It is important to follow Paul's thinking: When he found out that they did not know about the Spirit, his first thought was that there must have been some problem with their baptism. For Paul, there was an intimate connection between water and Spirit baptism. If they had been baptized, they should have the Spirit. However, it is even possible to be baptized—in ignorance—and not receive everything the Lord has for you. They had only been baptized in John's baptism, a baptism of repentance.

4 Paul said, "John's baptism was a baptism of repentance. He told the people to believe in the one coming after him, that is, in Jesus." 5 On hearing this, they were baptized in the name of the Lord Jesus.

There is biblical support for being baptized again! If you were baptized as a baby or without really accepting Jesus, you can be baptized a second time.

Correcting the problem

6 When Paul placed his hands on them, the Holy Spirit came on them, and they spoke in tongues and prophesied.

When we follow the New Testament model, we should experience similar results:

  1. They were baptized in water.

2. Paul laid hands on them. There is power in the laying on of hands, and God often uses it to impart the Holy Spirit.
3. The Holy Spirit came on them.
4. They spoke in tongues – and prophesied. The coming of the Spirit is almost always accompanied by some proclamation from our mouths: praise, new tongues, and, in this case, prophecy (probably more closely resembling the ecstatic prophesying spoken of in the Old Testament than giving prophetic messages).

Has the Spirit come on you? On your church? Has there been evidence of it? Have you been baptized in water? Are there people you need to lay hands on, with faith that God wants to fill them with the Spirit?

The growth of the church
7 There were about twelve men in all.

This was a small church, but don't despise the day of small beginnings. The number has special significance: With twelve disciples, Jesus changed the world, and God raised up a powerful church in Ephesus from these twelve. The number is not important; it is the anointing and unity of the brothers that releases God's power. When the Spirit comes, as it did here, you can expect growth. Look at what happened at Pentecost. Your church may not be very big, but don't let that discourage you. Don't be intimidated by mega-churches. Your church will grow, and God will do great things to glorify his name. If, for some reason, it stubbornly refuses to grow, you may need to evaluate if the Spirit is present in his fullness.

8 Paul entered the synagogue and spoke boldly there for three months, arguing persuasively about the kingdom of God. 9 But some of them became obstinate; they refused to believe and publicly maligned the Way. So Paul left them. He took the disciples with him and had discussions daily in the lecture hall of Tyrannus. ¹⁰ This went on for two years, so that all the Jews and Greeks who lived in the province of Asia heard the word of the Lord.

¹¹ God did extraordinary miracles through Paul, ¹² so that even handkerchiefs and aprons that had touched him were taken to the sick, and their illnesses were cured and the evil spirits left them.

This is amazing, and serves as a great example of how to plant a church or enter into a new field. Is anything like this happening in your church?

- **Public proclamation of Jesus Christ**. We go first to people who have some knowledge of the Word; usually, some of them are hungering for the truth. Here, Paul started at the synagogue.
- **Rejection and persecution**. You can count on it! But instead of giving up, they just moved to a school or a lecture hall. Sometimes we need to separate from those who do not accept the truth of the Word.
- **Boldness**. Paul spoke boldly.
- **Perseverance**. They were there every day for two years!
- **Arguing persuasively about the kingdom of God**. How much do you speak about the kingdom? It was a central theme in Jesus' teaching, especially in the Gospel of Matthew. Unfortunately, today we often hear more about men's kingdoms than God's kingdom.
- **Saturation**. The whole province heard the word. Can you say the same of your city?
- **Signs and wonders confirming the Word**. God did extraordinary miracles through Paul: Sickness was healed, and demons were cast out. It was the same in

Jesus' ministry and throughout the book of Acts. How about your ministry?

Do you think God could do the same thing today? Do you think he wants to? Why not? God wants to glorify Himself!

Many people are suffering under demonic oppression. Sickness abounds despite the massive amounts we spend on medical care. What do you think would happen if your church became known as a place where people regularly found healing? How about some of the most notorious sinners in your community getting free of their demons and being transformed by the power of Christ?

20

How Paul Ran His Race

Acts 20:17–38

¹⁷From Miletus, Paul sent to Ephesus for the elders of the church.

We left Paul during a tremendous time of ministry in Ephesus, but, as happened so often, he caused an uproar. In this case, it was not the Jews, but the threat he posed to the worship of Diana and the money it brought to the local craftsmen. He left Ephesus and traveled through Greece and Macedonia on his way to Syria, and then on to Jerusalem. He wanted to meet with the elders of the Ephesian church one last time, and like Jesus in the upper room (Jn. 14–16), he shared the deepest things of his heart, which have much to teach us about church leadership. This is the only discourse in Acts directed to believers—the rest are all evangelistic.

A transparent life

¹⁸ When they arrived, he said to them: "You know how I lived the whole time I was with you, from the first day I came into the province of Asia.

Paul was strikingly consistent. From the day he met them, he maintained an outstanding testimony. How about you? It makes

191

life and ministry much easier if people know what to expect from you. Paul had nothing to hide. His life was an open book, and they knew it well. His conscience was clear. Can your church and family say that about you? Is your life transparent?

[19] I served the Lord with great humility and with tears and in the midst of severe testing by the plots of my Jewish opponents.

Trials and tears
Paul was one of the greatest apostles, yet his life was hard and full of severe testing. If Paul was tested, chances are you will be too, and the testing may come from unexpected places. In his case, it was fellow Jews; for you, it could be family, church, or peers. Life is not easy.

- What are the tests in your life right now? Do you still keep serving the Lord? Do not allow the testing to discourage you.
- Testing usually humbles you. Paul had been a very proud Pharisee, but God humbled him. Serve Christ with humility. Reread Philippians 2 to see the humility that Jesus modeled. Can you say your ministry is characterized by humility?
- We can understand humility, but tears? Those tears reflected Paul's passion, his great love for the people, and the hours he spent agonizing in prayer. When someone is moved to tears as they minister over you, you know it is coming from the heart.

Teach publicly and house-to-house
[20] You know that I have not hesitated (AMP: did not shrink) to preach anything that would be helpful to you but have taught you publicly and from house to house.

If you receive something from the Lord that can help others, share it. Do not hesitate to preach; people need God's Word. Teach publicly, but also visit people in their homes and share the Word there. Years ago, it was customary for pastors to visit church members at home. Now it is rare, but they need that personal ministry.

Preach Christ to everyone

21 I have declared to both Jews and Greeks that they must turn to God in repentance and have faith in our Lord Jesus.

Along with preaching the Word, Paul was passionate about evangelism. Do not limit yourself to one group—preach Jesus to everyone. Paul's preaching focused on the need for repentance and belief in Jesus and his work of salvation.

Compelled by the Spirit

22 "And now, compelled by the Spirit, I am going to Jerusalem, not knowing what will happen to me there.

Everybody wants the anointing, the joy, and the gifts of the Spirit, but the same Spirit may lead us to do difficult things. To receive that guidance, you need an intimate relationship with him. When was the last time you felt *compelled* by the Spirit to do something? For Paul to go to a dangerous place required clear leading. If the Spirit directs you to go, obey. When you are compelled, you cannot ignore it. Do you have the faith to obey the Lord like Abraham (Genesis 12) and Phillip (Acts 9), without knowing all the details? We trust in the Lord for the future, not knowing what awaits us.

Prison and hardships

23 I only know that in every city the Holy Spirit warns me that prison and hardships are facing me.

One thing he did know: The Spirit not only led him, but he also warned him. Wherever he went, prison and hardships awaited him. Would you be excited about that? He did not mention offerings, success, love, or blessings. It was prison and hardships. Many would say, "Thanks, but I don't want that calling. I'll do something else." It is not easy to walk like a crucified Lord walked.

24 However, I consider my life worth nothing to me; my only aim is to finish the race and complete the task the Lord Jesus has given me—the task of testifying to the good news of God's grace.

Paul ran the race well. He knew the course—it had been revealed to him at conversion. He had preached to thousands and planted many churches. And you? Do you know what task God has given you? How is it going? Can you look hardship and death in the face, truly feeling that your life is worth nothing to you? Or are you still all about yourself?

Paul did not mention it here, and it was not his primary motive, but at the end of the race, a prize awaited him.

None of them will see him again
25 "Now I know that none of you among whom I have gone about preaching the kingdom will ever see me again. 26 Therefore, I declare to you today that I am innocent of the blood of any of you. 27 For I have not hesitated to proclaim to you the whole will of God.

- Paul knew little about the future, but he did know that none of them would see him again. Fortunately, he shared the whole will of God with them. That is impressive! Are you comprehensive in your preaching? Or do you ignore uncomfortable parts of God's will?

- Like Jesus, the focus of his preaching was the kingdom. Not an earthly kingdom of power and wealth, but a heavenly kingdom of righteousness, peace, and joy in the Holy Spirit. From the previous verse, we know it was also a message of grace.

- By faithfully preaching the Word, Paul knew he was innocent of anyone's blood. If he failed to preach to someone God directed him to, their blood would be on him (Ez. 3:20–21). Are you guilty of anyone's blood?

The pastors' responsibilities

[28] *Keep watch over* (AMP: *Take care of*) *yourselves and all the flock of which the Holy Spirit has made you overseers. Be shepherds of the church of God, which he bought with his own blood.*

Elders, pastors, and bishops are all words used for those who have authority in the church. They must:

- Keep careful watch over their own lives to make sure they are not in sin and are walking closely with the Lord. They need to take care of themselves physically, emotionally, and spiritually. Many pastors fail to do this, often neglecting relationships with family and friends. We tend to want others to take care of us, but part of being a mature leader is learning to take care of your own life. Keep yourself from sin and maintain your communion with the Lord.

- Tend the flock God has given them like a shepherd. That involves hard work; the pastor is responsible for the well-being of the church.

- Be called by The Holy Spirit. They did not volunteer for the job, nor were they elected. They do not have a choice of whether to do it or not. If you are in church leadership, has the Holy Spirit called you there? It is a heavy responsibility. Make sure God has placed you there.

The church is not theirs; it is God's. He paid a high price for it—the blood of Jesus. Be careful of acting like it is *your* church.

An interesting note for those who say the Bible does not say that Jesus is God: Paul says that Jesus' blood is God's own blood.

Wolves will come

29 I know that after I leave, savage wolves will come in among you and will not spare the flock.

Despite his hard work and God's care for his flock, the church was in danger. It was not just a possibility, Paul *knows* that savage wolves will come to destroy it. Wolves often come walking right in, since most churches are not prepared for them. Are you? In your own life? Your family? Your church? Are there savage wolves in your church right now? How are you responding to them?

They stayed away while the apostle was around. It is when the pastor or apostle is gone that they see their chance and jump on it. Be very careful of those times when spiritual authority is not present in the church.

False teachers

30 Even from your own number men will arise and distort the truth in order to draw away disciples after them.

The threat is not only external: Trusted brothers from within the church will try to steal your sheep with lies and false doctrines. They will attempt to influence people and make them their own disciples instead of forming them into disciples of Jesus Christ. Do you know what is being taught in the classes and groups in your church? What are you doing to make sure the doctrine is sound?

How do you handle false doctrine? Be on the lookout for those who would try to establish their own kingdom.

How do you think someone might distort the truth to attract followers? Maybe promises of prosperity, health, and blessings? Maybe conveniently avoiding talk of repentance and holiness? Or the cost of discipleship?

Laboring day and night

31 So be on your guard! Remember that for three years I never stopped warning each of you night and day with tears.

I am amazed at the love and passion Paul had for each person. His ministry was personal . No TV. No internet. No mega church. He taught in their churches, but every spare moment was spent with individuals. If you want to protect your flock from wolves and heretical teaching, you need to know and speak with each individual. If your church is big, make sure you have enough elders for that ministry. Yes, it takes a lot of time and work. What has happened to the tears? Where is the true love and passion for the Lord's work? Paul did this night and day! The elders may have to cut back on going to the movies and other forms of entertainment.

There is no time to kick back or let your defenses down. Wake up! Be on your guard! The devil is prowling around like a roaring lion looking for which church he can devour next.

The church entrusted to God

32 "Now I commit you to God and to the word of his grace, which can build you up and give you an inheritance among all those who are sanctified.

The time will come when the founding pastor leaves for another church, or heaven. Or the apostle leaves. You have done your best. Now you have to commit the church to God.

Paul's confidence came from his knowledge of God's grace. Many of us have an exaggerated sense of our own importance. It is God's grace that has the power to build you up and ensure you of your inheritance so that you can take your place with the rest of the sanctified.

Are you experiencing God's grace in your life? Do you need to be built up? Is this message of grace part of your ministry? Do you trust in God and his power to build up the brothers in your church?

Silver and gold

33 I have not coveted anyone's silver or gold or clothing.

I don't think we have a big problem today with pastors coveting their sheep's clothing, but their silver and gold is another story. To their shame and condemnation, many are stealing from their flock. And the sin is not just stealing, but also coveting. Be very careful of coveting and abusing Jesus' sheep for your own benefit.

34 You yourselves know that these hands of mine have supplied my own needs and the needs of my companions.

No one could ever accuse Paul of laziness. He worked tirelessly in the ministry, as well as his tent-making, so he would not have to ask anyone for anything. In that way, he provided not only for his own needs, but also those of his co-workers. How many "apostles" today work so that their co-workers are free to minister full-time? We know the Bible teaches that a church is responsible for paying its ministers, but Paul chose not to utilize that privilege to avoid being a stumbling block to anyone.

35 In everything I did, I showed you that by this kind of hard work we must help the weak, remembering the words the Lord Jesus himself said: 'It is more blessed to give than to receive.' "

Many pastors are underpaid as they serve their flocks, but, sadly, some enter the ministry thinking about what they can receive, whether money or power. God's servants do whatever they can to help the needy, never trying to take the little money they may have.

Our lives should be characterized by giving, not thinking about what we can get. That is how we experience God's blessing. Teach it to your children and model it in your church. Most people today think about what they can get. How about you?

Goodbye

36 When Paul had finished speaking, he knelt down with all of them and prayed. 37 They all wept as they embraced him and kissed him. 38 What grieved them most was his statement that they would never see his face again. Then they accompanied him to the ship.

There was a tremendous, affectionate bond between Paul and those he worked with. He was their spiritual father. Tears, hugs, and kisses all expressed that love.

Paul was a man of prayer. It was an important part of his ministry. Is it an integral part of yours?

These few verses are full of principles to use in your ministry. What do you need to put into practice? What is God's word for you in this passage?

21

Hope in Your Storm

Acts 27:7–44

Are you going through a storm? Or, even worse, have you suffered a shipwreck? It can even happen to someone full of the Holy Spirit and walking like Jesus walked—even the apostle Paul, traveling to Rome as a prisoner. This story reminds me of many inmates and their experiences as they were transported by bus or plane (called "Con Air" in the US). These final chapters of Acts could easily be a movie.

Chapter 27 opens with Paul, his companions, and other prisoners on a ship. The guard, Julius, kindly allowed Paul to visit his friends in the port city of Sidon. As they set sail, they immediately encountered many problems:

⁷ We had several days of slow sailing, and after great difficulty we finally neared Cnidus. But the wind was against us, so we sailed across to Crete and along the sheltered coast of the island, past the cape of Salmone. ⁸ We struggled along the coast with great difficulty and finally arrived at Fair Havens, near the town of Lasea. ⁹ We had lost a lot of time. The weather was becoming dangerous for sea travel because it was so late in the fall, and Paul spoke to the ship's officers about it. (NLT)

Everything was against them:

- It was slow sailing.
- They proceeded with great difficulty.
- The wind was against them.
- They struggled.
- They lost a lot of time.
- The weather was dangerous for sea travel.

Does it remind you of your life sometimes? Does it seem like you are getting nowhere? Is everything you do a struggle? Do you keep going, but with great difficulty? Is the wind against you, as the disciples experienced on the lake when Jesus came walking to them on the waters? Have you wasted a lot of time? Is your way dangerous?

Paul wanted to go to Rome and preach the gospel. He was anointed by God, one of the most important apostles in all of history, but God did not make it easy for him. Some preach that if you only have faith, there will be no headwinds or difficulties along the way, but the Bible teaches something different. Read Jesus' life again, and Paul's experiences on his missionary journeys.

On this trip, like some of their previous trips, they had to change their plans due to unfavorable conditions, and eventually they arrived at Fair Havens. Finally, something that sounded good! But it was not so good—it was not suitable for wintering. What could they do? God gave Paul the prisoner a word:

[10] *"Men, I can see that our voyage is going to be disastrous and bring great loss to ship and cargo, and to our own lives also."*

If God gives you a word, even if you are a prisoner, share it— unless God makes clear it is only for you. There is a great need for true prophets to warn this world of the coming judgment and disaster if it continues on its wrong path. But today, as then, most people do not want to hear the word of God. The centurion gave more credit to the helmsman and the ship's owner, and followed the majority. But many times the majority is wrong! If God warns you of danger, listen to him!

Verse 13 says "*they thought they could make it*" (NLT) when a gentle south wind began to blow. Contrary to the word of God, and according to appearances and the world's wisdom, people believe they can get what they want, but it is a deception. They can end up in perilous places, because we do not control the elements. Here, the weather changed. Soon a hurricane-force wind came up, a northeaster. This is how Luke described it:

[14] But the weather changed abruptly, and a wind of typhoon strength (called a "northeaster") burst across the island and blew us out to sea. [15] The sailors couldn't turn the ship into the wind, so they gave up and let it run before the gale.

[16] We sailed along the sheltered side of a small island named Cauda, where with great difficulty we hoisted aboard the lifeboat being towed behind us. [17] Then the sailors bound ropes around the hull of the ship to strengthen it. They were afraid of being driven across to the sandbars of Syrtis off the African coast, so they lowered the sea anchor to slow the ship and were driven before the wind.

[18] The next day, as gale-force winds continued to batter the ship, the crew began throwing the cargo overboard. [19] The following day they even took some of the ship's gear and threw it overboard. [20] The terrible storm raged for many days, blotting out the sun and the stars, until at last all hope was gone.

[21] No one had eaten for a long time. Finally, Paul called the crew together and said, "Men, you should have listened to me in the

first place and not left Crete. You would have avoided all this damage and loss. (NLT)

- The boat could not handle the tempest, so they gave up and let it run with the wind.
- They could barely hold onto the lifeboat.
- They began to throw the cargo overboard.
- The storm blotted out the sun and stars for many days.
- The storm kept raging.
- All hope was gone.
- They had not eaten for a long time

It does not say what the brothers did during those days, but I am sure they were praying and helping others. In this ordeal, I am confident that they, more than anyone else, kept their strength and hope. However, fourteen days passed (v. 27) without receiving any word from the Lord. Do you know what it is like to be in a storm so big that it seems like you are going to die, and you do not get answers to your prayers? It feels like the storm will never end. Day after day, you are struggling just to survive.

21 After they had gone a long time without food, Paul stood up before them and said: "Men, you should have taken my advice not to sail from Crete; then you would have spared yourselves this damage and loss. 22 But now I urge you to keep up your courage, because not one of you will be lost; only the ship will be destroyed. 23 Last night an angel of the God to whom I belong and whom I serve stood beside me 24 and said, 'Do not be afraid, Paul. You must stand trial before Caesar; and God has graciously given you the lives of all who sail with you.' 25 So keep up your courage, men, for I have faith in God that it will happen just as he told me. 26 Nevertheless, we must run aground on some island."

The sailors were finally ready to listen to God's word, and God sent an angel to Paul. Imagine seeing an angel in that situation! Paul told them the words that no man wants to hear: You should have followed my advice. If we keep God's word, we can avoid great loss, but God can redeem even that situation, especially if there is someone like Paul on board.

The first word the angel gave Paul was: Do not be afraid. Even Paul was afraid! It is God's word to you in your storm now. God has plans for you. You may suffer loss in the process (here they lost the boat and all the cargo), but many years ago I learned that God does not care that much if we lose money and material things; he can always give you more money. Your life is worth more than money.

Finally, after two weeks, they found themselves near an island, and the sailors wanted to abandon ship:

30 In an attempt to escape from the ship, the sailors let the lifeboat down into the sea, pretending they were going to lower some anchors from the bow.

However, Paul (who received it by revelation, since he was not a sailor) told the centurion that if they did not stay on the ship, the others would not be saved, and this time the centurion listened to him. God had given authority to Paul the prisoner. It reminds me of Joseph and his authority in the Egyptian prison. In the same way, God will give you authority in your prison or work.

33 Just before dawn Paul urged them all to eat. "For the last fourteen days," he said, "you have been in constant suspense and have gone without food—you haven't eaten anything. 34 Now I urge you to take some food. You need it to survive. Not one of you will lose a single hair from his head." 35 After he said this, he took some bread and gave thanks to God in front of them all. Then he broke it and began to eat. ³⁶ They were all encouraged and ate some food themselves. ³⁷ Altogether there were 276 of us on board. ³⁸ When they had eaten as much as they wanted, they lightened the ship by throwing the grain into the sea.

Paul was so confident that he encouraged everyone to eat. He thanked God in front of them, took bread, and broke it, just as Jesus had fed the multitude. God wants to use you to encourage and bless everyone around you. Sometimes you have to get up and bless them and break the bread of life.

⁴² The soldiers planned to kill the prisoners to prevent any of them from swimming away and escaping. ⁴³ But the centurion wanted to spare Paul's life and kept them from carrying out their plan. He ordered those who could swim to jump overboard first and get to land. ⁴⁴ The rest were to get there on planks or on other pieces of the ship. In this way everyone reached land safely.

Once again, God saved Paul. He still has a long way to go, but for the moment, Paul and everyone on that ship were fine. I pray that in your storm now, everyone in your company—all your family—would arrive on dry land, safe and sound. God gives us times of rest and blessing before entering the ship again, perhaps to find yourself in another storm, but your Father wants to teach you that even in the storm he has everything under control. Each storm is another opportunity for God to display his power. If there is never a storm, you do not need God. As Jesus said to his disciples when he rebuked the wind: *Why are you so afraid? Do you still have no faith?* (Mrk. 4:40) You may be in a storm now, but Jesus has authority over the wind and the waves, and he has given you that authority. Be strong and courageous.

Conclusion

Do you remember the controversy in the first chapter of Acts? Was it wrong to select Matthias as a replacement for Judas?

I believe Paul was God's selection to replace him. We end with another controversy, this time about Paul: Was it right for him to go to Jerusalem despite the warnings of danger?

Most of the final chapters of Acts (which I do not include in this study) surround his journey to Jerusalem, his arrest and imprisonment, and his arrival in Rome. When he left the elders of Ephesus, Acts 20:38 says: *What grieved them most was his statement that they would never see his face again.*

After saying goodbye, they sailed to Tyre: *We sought out the disciples there and stayed with them seven days. Through the Spirit they urged Paul not to go on to Jerusalem. When it was time to leave, we left and continued on our way* (AMP: ***But** when our time there was ended, we left and proceeded on our journey,* Acts 21: 4–5). The "but" (which is not included in all translations) indicates that Paul ignored their warning, given *"through the Spirit."* To me, it seems unwise not to wait, pray, and seek confirmation of God's will, but we know that Paul could be stubborn.

From Tyre, after a day with the brothers in Ptolemais, they reached Caesarea, and the house and church of Philip the evangelist. Here, the warning seems even stronger:

After we had been there a number of days, a prophet named Agabus came down from Judea. Coming over to us, he took Paul's belt, tied his own hands and feet with it and said, "The Holy Spirit says, 'In this way the Jewish leaders in Jerusalem will bind the owner of this belt and will hand him over to the Gentiles.'"

When we heard this, we and the people there pleaded with Paul not to go up to Jerusalem. Then Paul answered, "Why are you weeping and breaking my heart? I am ready not only to be bound, but also to die in Jerusalem for the name of the Lord Jesus." When he would not be dissuaded, we gave up and said, "The Lord's will be done." (Acts 21:10–14)

I am impressed that God sent this prophet with a very clear message. All Paul's traveling companions and the brothers in the church begged him not to go to Jerusalem, although the prophet did not say that he should not go, only what was going to happen there. But Paul is determined: He has to go to Jerusalem, and his ultimate goal was Rome. We probably all know someone stubborn; once their mind is made up, they will not change for anything. Was God calling him to go there? It never says, and it is up to us to decide whether Paul was correct. At first glance, the fruits (arrest, shipwreck, and probably death) do not seem very good. However, in the process, he preached to many people and got to Rome.

What do you think?

Is it possible for us, through a foolish decision, to cut short the ministry or the life that God has planned for us? Or, given God's sovereignty, is it impossible to change his plan?

Two things complicate the decision:

- Acts 20:22 23: "And now, compelled by the Spirit (NLT: bound by the Spirit, AMP: compelled by the Spirit and obligated by my convictions), *I am going to Jerusalem, not knowing what will happen to me there. I only know that in every city the Holy Spirit warns me that prison and hardships are facing me.* At first, it seems that the Holy Spirit forced him to go to Jerusalem, against the warnings of prophets and other brothers. However, the translation from the Greek is difficult, which is noted in the Amplified Bible, Classic Edition: *bound by the [Holy] Spirit and obligated and compelled by the [convictions of my own] spirit.* It is unclear if the "spirit" here is the Holy Spirit or Paul's own spirit. I have known enough great men of God to know how easy it is to deceive yourself, especially after experiencing success and fame. They may sincerely believe that it is the voice of the Holy Spirit, when in reality they are "bound in spirit," with an urgency to fulfill what is in *their* "spirit." Could it be that God sent the prophets to tell him he was wrong?

- A word that came to Paul after his trial in Jerusalem: *"The following night the Lord stood near Paul and said, "Take courage! As you have testified about me in Jerusalem, so you must also testify in Rome"* (Acts 23:11). Does this mean it was God's plan from the start? Or, at that point, despite a possible "mistake," that God would redeem the situation and open doors to witness in these cities?

There are times when we complicate the situation for ourselves, like Paul appealing to Caesar. King Agrippa said to Festus, the governor: *"This man could have been set free if he had not appealed to Caesar"* (Acts 26:32).

As with the "mistake" in the first chapter, I am not dogmatic, and I believe that both are possible. But from what I have observed in many situations, I tend to think that Paul missed the opportunity for a more extended ministry because of his stubbornness. We may be in situations where we see danger and warn a servant of God to seek more confirmation from the Lord before making a decision, but he has free will, and we have to leave him in God's hands, as Paul's companions said in Acts 21:14: *The Lord's will be done!*

Will you write the next volume?

The book of Acts ends with these words: *For two whole years Paul stayed there in his own rented house and welcomed all who came to see him. He proclaimed the kingdom of God and taught about the Lord Jesus Christ—with all boldness and without hindrance!* (Acts 28:30–31).

It seems to me that the book needs at least one more chapter. Perhaps it was at this point that Luke finished, but there are many details we just do not know: When and how did Paul die? Did he make the trip to Spain as he hoped to? Some legends say he did. Just as it seems that the book ends prematurely, it seems that there should have been a couple more chapters in Paul's life. But perhaps it is up to us to finish the book of Acts, and God allowed it to end that way on purpose.

This is my conclusion of this series, "Walk like Jesus walked." After months of writing, I am more convinced than ever that the center of the Christian life is just that simple. There are so many things happening in the church and the world, but that goal keeps me focused. It is a thrill to walk like Christ.

Now it is your turn. You write the next volume in this series. It would be great to have hundreds of volumes of testimonies from brothers and sisters who are walking as Jesus walked! Tales of God's power to make disciples and extend the kingdom throughout the world. I trust I will be there and see you among those whom Jesus says *will walk with me, dressed in white, for they are worthy* (Rev. 3:4). Then we will truly walk like Jesus walks.

www.ingramcontent.com/pod-product-compliance
Lightning Source LLC
Chambersburg PA
CBHW060237050426
42448CB00009B/1484